Chosen for Paradise

Reframing Election in Romans 9-11

By John Crowder

The Inclusion of Humanity
In the Saving Act of Jesus

Sons of Thunder Ministries & Publications
Portland, Oregon

Chosen for Paradise by John Crowder

Published by:
Sons of Thunder Ministries & Publications
P.O. Box 40
Marylhurst, OR 97036

www.thenewmystics.com
Phone: **1-877-343-3245**
Email: info@thenewmystics.org

This book or parts thereof may not be reproduced in any form, stored in a retrieval system or transmitted in any form by any means – electronic, mechanical, photocopy, recording or otherwise – without prior written permission of the publisher, except as provided by United States of America copyright law.

Copyright © 2014 by John Crowder
All rights reserved

Library of Congress Control Number: 2014919759
International Standard Book Number: 978-0-9770826-5-0

Printed in the United States of America

9 8 7 6 5 4 3 2 1

This book is dedicated to all the children of our homes in India.

"Do not be afraid, little flock, for your Father has been pleased to give you the kingdom." – Luke 12:32

Contents

Translation Index   7
Bible Translations :: Versions Used

Preface   9
Author's Note :: Opening Thoughts and Credits
by John Crowder

Introduction   13
The Most Important Election Ever :: Gleaning from Karl Barth
by Dr. Eric Wilding

Section One   21
The Election of Jesus Christ :: Beyond Free Will vs. Sovereignty
The Predestination & Inclusion of Humanity

Section Two   49
Vessels of Honor and Wrath :: The Lie of Double Predestination
Does a Sovereign God Choose People to Burn?

Epilogue   83
Chosen for Paradise :: The Eternal Plan of God
Better Than Eden

The Text   89
Romans 9-11 :: Scripture Reference From the NIV

Translation Index

The Bible translations in this book can be identified by the following codes when used:

BCJ – The Heart of Paul: A Relational Paraphrase of the New Testament (Waco, TX: Word Books, 1976). Ben Campbell Johnson.
DRB – *Douay-Rheims Bible 1582-1609* (Fitzwilliam, NH: Loreto Publications, 2007).
ESV – *The English Standard Version Bible: Containing the Old and New Testaments with Apocrypha* (Oxford: Oxford University Press, 2009).
KJV – *The Holy Bible King James Version: 1611 Edition.*
LXX – *The Septuagint Translation* in modern English.
NIV – *The Holy Bible, New International Version* (Grand Rapids: The Zondervan Corporation, 1973, 1978, 1984). International Bible Society.
WAND – *The New Testament Letters* (New York: Oxford University Press, 1950). J.W.C. Wand.

Most verses listed without translation references are partially quoted or inferred, or are taken from the New International Version.

Preface

Such a heavy topic like that of predestination can go one of two ways. Many theologians take the route of writing thick, voluminous tomes guaranteed to collect more dust than readers. To bolster credibility, they prefer to fill every square millimeter of open margin space with fine print footnotes referencing even older dead theologians than them themselves.

Every teacher is tempted to blather on longer than he should for the sheer joy of listening to himself talk. I am not immune from this lure myself. I half ashamedly admit that one of my books had 20 pages of references alone. But even I have my limits. And in this work, I have chosen to take a different route. When dealing with a doctrine that has caused more theological cat fighting than any other for the past 500 years, perhaps it is simplicity that will calm the storm. And so this book is intentionally rather short – a booklet if you will. Please do not mistake its brevity for lack of study or scholastic aptitude, though I am admittedly a dropout with no degrees framed on my wall. What I forfeit in irrelevant footnotes I hope to compensate in reader accessibility. I have read enough of those dusty books to appreciate a brief explanation.

The fact is that the average fellow, not the high theological society, is most appreciative of clarity. Theologians generally thrive on confusing themselves - God forbid they make anything easy for anyone else.

The subject of election or predestination – God's *choosing* if you will – is really a rather simple one. It is all summarized in the person of Jesus Christ. The electing God and the elected man are One in the same. God Almighty chose His Son on behalf of the human race. But we have overcomplicated this subject with human logic and a humanistic focus. In the one camp, our Calvinist brothers believe that God chooses one human being over the other. One destined to Paradise, the other destined to

PREFACE

bake forever in the flames of Hell. In the other camp, our Arminian brothers believe that man himself must choose God. Ultimately, it is man's decision, not God's decision that saves him. Whether it is our willpower, our choice or our ability to muster up the work of faith (how much faith is enough?), the Arminian surely implies that mankind on some level saves himself. Human willpower becomes at least one link in the chain of salvation; therefore, the entire chain becomes as flimsy as it's weakest link. *Man must save himself.*

I do not think it an inappropriate caricature to summarize each side's position on the topic. After all, we are keeping this short. Heaven knows you need to return to your emails, web streaming and Sunday afternoon football.

But before I bring this introduction to a close, I should mention one other camp that Christendom loves to shun – *the Universalists*. Because I fall outside the boundaries of the two leading aforementioned groups, I am often confused for a member of this latter camp.

At least the Christian Universalists can see the strong, Biblical Pauline doctrine that all of humanity was included in the saving act of Jesus. But their focus likewise devolves into logic and humanism - mostly revolving incessantly around the topic of Hell. They become dogmatic on their claims about the afterlife – asserting that the bad place doesn't exist or that it is unpopulated altogether. While I empathize with their frustration over the maniacal Calvinist god and the impotent Arminian one, I believe my Universalist brother too quickly resigns himself to an ideal at the expense of Scripture.

I believe there is a better course to take. It begins with the heart of the Trinity. Not the Calvinist "trinity" of Demon, Son and Holy Bible. But a loving Father who forever desired to weave humanity into His loving relationship with His Son in the power and presence of a very real, tangible Holy Ghost. Not the Arminian "trinity" that sits aloof until we invite it into our hearts

PREFACE

with tears at the altar. But a present Father whose Son stepped into our humanity and poured His Spirit out on all flesh before ever asking our permission.

Theology is not information. It all begins and finds its ultimate consummation in this love relationship of the Trinity. Anything outside this face-to-face intimacy between Father, Son and Spirit - this other-giving love that spilled over to humanity, is not the God of the Bible. Our understanding of the doctrine of election comes into alignment only when we begin to comprehend the relational love of God. God is Family. And we have all been grafted into that family, even if we want to act like prodigal bastards and stand outside the gates of Heaven that are forever open day and night, sulking and burning in the remorse and guilt that He never chose to heap upon us. We have the freedom to reject Him all we want, but we are still included from His end of the relationship.

Finally, let me explain that the material in this volume was originally part of my larger book *Cosmos Reborn*. I recommend reading this as an addendum to that longer work. But for an all-encompassing scope of Christ's redemptive act, I advise you to read that one, which offers a fuller, robust understanding of the role of faith, the new birth and our effortless inclusion in the vicarious, incarnational humanity of the Son of Man. In *Cosmos Reborn*, I also give an exhaustive treatment on the subject of Hell, judgment, wrath and other such cheery topics that I cannot begin to cover in depth here. It's a book of deep subject matter in everyday lingo that offers a complete reformatting of many evangelical doctrines around the central revelation of the person and finished work of Jesus. Funny how our doctrines all go wobbly when we realize Jesus actually accomplished something. And moreover when we see how much we've underestimated Him.

I thank Dr. C. Baxter Kruger for his insightful editing to chop these chapters on election out of that already swollen book ... yet again to make things more approachable to the average

PREFACE

reader. By no means is this book a gathering of post-edit scraps that didn't make *Cosmos Reborn*. On the contrary, the subject of election is such a vital, yet misunderstood doctrine, that it merits its own rendering here. To fully plunge into Romans nine through eleven, which we are about to do, required a few lobes of mental focus that would have sent too much voltage through the already maxed circuit boards of *Cosmos Reborn* readers. Again, election is a rather simple topic. We've just overcomplicated it to the degree that we must take a little time to disassemble the existing duct-taped doctrinal monstrosity that wasn't wired to code by modern evangelicalism.

And finally, credit is due to the pioneering genius of Karl Barth, Thomas F. Torrance and the many Trinitarian theologians who laid the groundwork in the West for returning to the roots of the authentic Good News proclaimed by the Church Fathers. Barth's understanding of election was an invaluable source of guidance for me in the following chapters.

In Him from the foundation of the world,

John Crowder

Introduction
BY DR. ERIC WILDING

Many theologians have attempted to grasp the mystery of election attested to in Scripture. One of the most influential commentators on the doctrine of election is the Swiss theologian Karl Barth. For Barth, the doctrine of election is the sum of the gospel and the foundation for understanding God.

God's Free Choice
"Election" simply means "a choice." The Christian doctrine of election involves a choice made by God. For Karl Barth, this doctrine – the decision of God before all time to be Who He is for humanity — is the basic truth on which all other Christian truths are built. The doctrine of election involves two aspects, the electing God and the elected man. As the electing God, the Father, the Son and the Holy Spirit together make a choice. The choice God makes is that the Son of God will become the elected man, Jesus of Nazareth.

The Triune God eternally elects, or chooses, in divine freedom, to be for humanity the God of grace and love. Therefore, in Jesus Christ, Who is fully God and fully man, God is both the Elector and the Elected. Barth writes, "In the midst of time it happened that God became man for our good. While underlining the uniqueness of this event, we have to reflect that this was not an accident, not one historical event among others. But it is the event which God willed from eternity."[1]

Theologian and Barth scholar John Webster describes it this way, "God elects to be this God, God in this man, God known in and as Jesus Christ."[2] As the act of grace and love, the Son of God is elected to give of Himself to become united with the

---

[1] Karl Barth, *Dogmatics in Outline* (Harper & Row: 1959), 69.
[2] John Webster, *Barth: Outstanding Christian Thinkers* (Continuum, 2000), 91.

INTRODUCTION

Son of Man for the specific purpose to save sinful humans. This is the act of free grace where God gives "love in the deepest condescension," that is, He reaches down to pull humans to Himself. The Son of God empties and humbles Himself so that humans may be united in fellowship with God (see Phi. 2:6-8; John 17:22-24).

This is the work of the Triune God: Father, Son and Spirit, in perfect love and perfect unity for the sake of humanity. Barth states, "This work of the Son of God includes the work of the Father as its presupposition and the work of the Holy Spirit as its consequence."[3] We know the Father loves us because we know Jesus loves us, and we live in this assurance by the Spirit.

Scripture tells us that God is love (1 John 4:8, 16). As the Triune God, the Father, Son and Holy Spirit have freely shared their perfect love and fellowship within the Godhead eternally, and by God's own free choice, He elects to share that same love with humanity through Jesus Christ, who is the elect man on behalf of all humanity.

How do we know about this choice? Barth explains, "It is grounded in the knowledge of Jesus Christ because He is both the electing God and elected man in One."[4] We only need to look to Jesus Christ to know about this election. Theologian Robert Jenson comments, "Jesus Christ is therefore the basis of the doctrine of election. All its statements must be statements about Him."[5]

Predestination
For Barth, predestination is identical with the election of Jesus Christ. God freely chooses or predestines Himself and all

---

[3] Barth, *Dogmatics in Outline*, 71.
[4] Karl Barth, *Church Dogmatics II/2* (T&T Clark, 2004), 3. All quotes, unless otherwise cited, come from this source.
[5] Robert W. Jenson, *Alpha and Omega: A Study in the Theology of Karl Barth* (Wipf & Stock, 2002), 144.

INTRODUCTION

humans to be in loving relationship with and through Jesus Christ. God will have it no other way; He loves humanity and will not be without humanity.

The problem is that humans were fallen, sinful beings who rejected God and needed redemption in order to stand in that fellowship from their side. Scripture testifies to God's foreknowledge – before creation – that human beings would be sinful and would be in need of redemption and reconciliation (see 1 Peter 1:18-21; Rev. 13:8; Rom. 5:6-11; 8:28-30; Eph. 1:3-14; Col. 1:15-20). Barth explains, "Yet these transgressors are the ones on whose behalf the eternal love of God for Jesus Christ is willed and extended."

You may say, "Predestination? Doesn't that mean that God accepted some (the elect) and rejected others (the reprobate) before He even created humanity?"

Barth challenges this hyper-Calvinist version of "double predestination" because of its lack of scriptural support. For Barth, God is not a capricious tyrant who elects some to salvation and elects others to perdition by some abstract absolute decree. On the contrary, all knowledge we have about God and His election is in and through Jesus Christ – there is nothing hidden beyond or behind that knowledge.

Double Predestination in Jesus Christ

For Barth, "double predestination" has to do with the election of Jesus Christ for crucifixion and resurrection. Before time began, God accepted all humanity by electing Jesus Christ in our place and on our behalf through the incarnation, the cross and the empty tomb.

At the crucifixion, God rejects and says NO to disordered human sin that caused alienation from Him. However, God's NO is not directed at us – even though we deserved it because of our rejection of God. Instead, Jesus takes the rejection and

INTRODUCTION

the NO of God totally upon Himself as the human representative of and substitute for all humanity.

The NO is absolutely necessary so that we can hear God's YES. Jesus Christ does not come to the world as "an accuser, as a prosecutor, as a judge, as an executioner." Instead He is "the herald of this Yes which God has spoken to it [the world]. ... God has loved it from all eternity, and ... He has put His love into action in the death of Jesus Christ."[6]

The resurrection of Jesus Christ is God's YES to Jesus Christ. It is the acceptance of Jesus Christ's obedient submission to God's will. In and through Jesus Christ, the YES of God is freely given to all human beings. Therefore, we may say that Jesus Christ is our elected representative.

You may ask, "What does the NO and YES mean for me?"

Theologian Joseph Mangina writes, God's No is "a death-dealing rejection of sin and evil" and Yes is "a life-giving affirmation of covenant love." The NO passed away at the cross; Jesus Christ bore the NO and totally removed it. There remains only the covenant or relationship of YES with the resurrection of Jesus Christ (see 2 Cor. 1:19-20).

Ultimately, double predestination involves Jesus dying for the sins of every human being who ever lived – not just a closed number of elect – so that all might have eternal life (see John 3:16-17; 1 Tim. 2:3-6; 2 Peter 3:9, 1 John 2:2). At the resurrection, the Father gave acceptance to Jesus Christ and everyone with Him. Barth states, "We have to see our own election in that of the man Jesus because His election includes ours within itself and because ours is grounded in His. We are elected together with Him in so far as we are elected 'in Him.'"

---

[6] Karl Barth, *Church Dogmatics IV/1*(T & T Clark, 1956), 347.

INTRODUCTION

The Good News

Barth calls the doctrine of election the sum of the gospel, for it reveals the heart of God: "God's eternal will is the election of Jesus Christ." He is the loving God who has freely chosen and created human beings to be in His image and in fellowship with Him. This is the absolute good news. There is no bad news mixed with the good news, no fear mixed with terror, no certainty mixed with uncertainty. We are not left to blind fate or some unknown will of God. Our election and predestination by God is certain in Jesus Christ, and in Him alone and in Him fully we have and know the will of God for the meaning and direction of our lives.

THE GREATER TRUTH

To pronounce the name of Jesus Christ means to acknowledge that we are cared for, that we are not lost. Jesus Christ is man's salvation in all circumstances and in face of all that darkens his life, including the evil that proceeds from himself. There is nothing which is not already made good in this happening, that God became man for our good. Anything that is left can be no more than the discovery of this fact. We do not exist in any kind of gloomy uncertainty; we exist through the God who was gracious to us before we existed at all. It may be true that we exist in contradiction to this God, that we live in remoteness from Him, indeed in hostility to Him. It is still truer that God has prepared reconciliation for us, before we entered the struggle against Him. And true though it may be that in connection with our alienation from God man can only be regarded as a lost being, it is still much truer that God has so acted for our good, does it and will also act, that there exists a salvation for every lost condition. It is this faith that we are called to belief through the Christian Church and in the Holy Spirit.

— Karl Barth, *Dogmatics in Outline*, page 71

SECTION 1. THE ELECTION OF JESUS CHRIST
BEYOND FREE WILL VS. SOVEREIGNTY

THE PREDESTINATION &
INCLUSION OF HUMANITY

The doctrine of election is the sum of the Gospel ...
He is both the electing God and elected man in One.
- Karl Barth

THE ELECTION OF JESUS CHRIST

It is one thing to believe that Christ died as a man. But it is altogether scandalous to believe He died as *humanity*.

To see the massive scope and cosmic ramification of the incarnation of Jesus challenges everything we thought we knew about the fate of mankind. It is not just that God was bound up in Christ ... but in Christ, He bound the entire created order to Himself. Something was utterly completed on behalf of the universe in His life, death and resurrection. "God was in Christ reconciling the cosmos to Himself" (2 Cor. 5:19).

As folks begin to consider the stunning scope of the finished work of the cross – particularly regarding the inclusion of all humanity in Christ – questions regarding the role of personal faith, the nature of the new birth, the wrath of God and ultimately the dynamics of Heaven and Hell begin to surface. And these should be revisited in light of scripture – not merely through the lens of modern evangelicalism. These important topics urged me to write, *Cosmos Reborn* in an effort to tackle the universal scope of Christ's saving act.

But along with all the above questions, we are also challenged to step back into a most misunderstood and volatile subject in theology ... the topic of *election* or *predestination*. Often framed as God's sovereign "choosing" of humanity either for bliss or torment, it is no wonder that theologians have battled over election for centuries; Karl Barth calls it "the sum of the Gospel." God's election is a vital concept to understand – but also the most debated and convoluted by theologians.

And that, dear reader, is exactly what we intend to explore in this short volume. Here we will focus strictly on predestination. In fact, our exploration of this subject may prompt you to investigate many of the aforementioned topics in a fresh light (the role of faith, the new birth, divine wrath, Hell, etc.).

THE ELECTION OF JESUS CHRIST

In the following pages I hope to simplify a deep subject for the casual reader – and I hope to challenge the "experts" who have already staked out their opinions.

In a nutshell, the common debate over election has always pitted two streams of thought over against one another: *Arminianism and Calvinism*. These may seem irrelevant to the average Christian whose primary spiritual concern is whether they've clocked in 15 minutes of prayer this morning. But how we think along these lines have massive ramifications to our worldview and how we live our day-to-day lives in relation to God. These theologies have set the course of entire societies, endorsed wars, slavery and molded the minds of men. Essentially, the argument revolves around this question, "Do we choose God, or does God choose us?" Like a nauseating merry-go-round, this never-ending squabble proved the most puzzling dilemma for those who swim the deepest waters of theology. The entire debate seemed locked into a question of our free will versus God's sovereign choice.

There are some radically depressing ideas that have infiltrated Christianity through this debate, which I hope to address by infusing some Good News – some Gospel Prozac. You may get a few monkey wrenches thrown into your theological cog work here. To think outside the box in areas we were told to *just accept* – no questions asked – may expose some so-called "dogmatic truths" to really be doctrines of demons. Just because scriptures are interpreted a certain way in Sunday school doesn't make it right. My goal is for you to be completely intoxicated on God's love and eradicate false doctrine that has sown fear and anxiety into your life. It will also cause you to see others in the way God truly sees them. I encourage you to remain teachable through these chapters – keep an open mind and *read the scriptures!* Paul commended the Bereans because they were teachable, but neither did they just bite off anything he said. They checked the scriptures and confirmed the truth.

THE ELECTION OF JESUS CHRIST

The Current Debate

As these two theologies evolved – Calvinism and Arminianism – it became clear that both contained truths. Yet the flaw in each one seems to be an inherent "human focus" that quickly overlooks the centrality of the person and work of Christ. Both traditions ultimately rely on a logic-based, humanistic linchpin.

For the Arminian, he rightly recognized that Christ died for all men – that God did not intentionally desire any of His creation to be destroyed. Therefore, the Arminian logically insisted that salvation must ultimately be a *human choice* – whether to accept or reject God's goodness in Christ. Salvation became about man's "personal decision" for Christ – a human response of the human will – to something that was available to all. Hence, the advent of the *altar call*, the *sinner's prayer*, etc. God gives a fair shot to everybody, but it's up to you to decide.

Arminianism mostly thrives in Charismatic and Pentecostal type circles where a strong focus is regularly placed on your personal application of the Gospel. Every service requires congregants to dig deep, recommit themselves, etc. Many circles also devolve into an internal strife to somehow "maintain" this salvation based on human decision/response to Jesus, so as not to lose it. A fear of not measuring up to a required human performance standard for salvation is prevalent and often debilitating.

The Calvinist, however, saw the fatal flaw in this concept. Salvation is not up to you. Your crooked, depraved willpower is incapable of "choosing God." In fact, it is God who must choose you. Faith is a gift, not something you drum up. If "my response" or "my decision" saves me, then I am boasting in human willpower – and therefore saving myself. Christ is not glorified, and I am adhering to my own striving, legal attempts to please God – rather than His grace. The Calvinist rightly shows that the Arminian version of God is impotent, lacking the power to overcome an individual's decision-making process. Any response we make to God is a byproduct of His earlier

THE ELECTION OF JESUS CHRIST

choice for us. *Free will* is the ultimate power broker for the Arminian – not the grace of God. Even for man to meet God "half-way" is an admission that Christ's work alone was not enough.

The Arminian Flaw

As a Charismatic, I was always a bit strange because I did not tow the party line in this area. Of course as a youngster, I was gripped with fear that my human performance did not merit keeping my salvation. But thanks to the influence of a Presbyterian friend – and moreover by a tangible encounter with the goodness of God in my teen years – the scriptures came alive to me regarding God's sovereignty in my salvation. As a Charismatic, I loved miracles, healing and spiritual gifts (and incalculably more I loved the tangible Presence of God). But I knew better than to ascribe to the Arminian, do-it-yourself mantra that most Charismatics and Pentecostals hold dearly. I knew that my own crooked willpower was incapable of *choosing God*, much less "keeping" Him. I didn't choose Him; He chose me (John 15:16). I did nothing to get my salvation, and it was not up to me to maintain it. Arminianism is chock-full of willpower and striving. My choice didn't save me; Jesus did. I knew that even my repentance didn't save me. Repentance is not the price tag for salvation; it is a fruit of salvation. Salvation is about His will – His choice to save.

Children of God are those, "who are born, not of blood, nor of the will of the flesh, nor of the will of man, but of God" (John 1:13, DRB).

> *Of His own will He brought us forth by the word of truth, that we should be a kind of first fruits of His creatures*
> (Jas. 1:18, ESV).

No willpower here. You were not saved because of your "decision for Christ" but because of His "decision for you." You were in His heart and imagination before the world was created. Not born of a human decision, but born from above.

THE ELECTION OF JESUS CHRIST

*Blessed be the God and Father of our Lord Jesus Christ, who hath blessed us with all spiritual blessings in heavenly places in Christ: according as **He hath chosen us in Him** before the foundation of the world, that we should be holy and without blame before Him in love: **Having predestinated us unto the adoption of children** by Jesus Christ to Himself, according to the **good pleasure of His will, to the praise of the glory of His grace**, wherein He hath **made us accepted in the beloved**. ... Having made known unto us the mystery of His will, according to His good pleasure **which He hath purposed in Himself**. ... In whom also we have obtained an inheritance, **being predestinated according to the purpose of Him who worketh all things after the counsel of His own will*** (Eph. 1:3-6, 11, KJV).

Now, when I read the above passage, I do not see my own human will in there anywhere. It is all about His predetermination – His prior choice and His accomplishment.

Free will is a misnomer. It sounds romantic, like Braveheart running through a field with flowers in his hair yelling "Freeeedom!" But there is really no freedom outside of God's will. Of course we all have a will. We make choices. I can take my kids to the Jelly Belly factory, and they can choose a red jelly bean or a green jelly bean. But who drove them to the Jelly Belly factory? Who is buying the jelly beans? Who is monitoring their sugar intake? At the end of the day, Dad is still sovereign.

Your own "separate" freedom is capable only of resisting God. As Charles Spurgeon said, "Free will has carried many souls to Hell, but never a soul to Heaven yet."[7] Your willpower cannot climb you up; it can only pull you down. You were not created for separateness. Freedom is not separateness. While there is a sense of distinction in the Persons of the Trinity, there is not an opposition of goals. "Not My will but Yours be done" speaks

---

[7] Charles Spurgeon, "Samson Conquered." (1858 Sermon).

THE ELECTION OF JESUS CHRIST

not of division but unity in the heart of the Trinity. The true emancipation of the will is realized when we see that His was always our deepest, if not hidden desire.

Human faith is so often preached as the "surcharge" for salvation. But faith is not willpower. Faith is effortless trust, and it is a gift. Faith has nothing to do with willpower – it is the opposite of willpower. I can never boast in my choosing. This was a core, lifelong message of Martin Luther. His book *Bondage of the Will was a cornerstone* for the Reformation. All the major reformers – Calvin, Zwingli, etc. agreed with him in his battle against what he called the "idol of the human will." It is the lie that our willpower has anything whatsoever to do with salvation. Spurgeon makes a brilliant statement:

> ... and I will go as far as Martin Luther, in that strong assertion of his, where he says, "If any man doth ascribe of salvation, even the very least, to the free will of man, he knoweth nothing of grace, and he hath not learnt Jesus Christ aright." It may seem a harsh sentiment; but he who in his soul believes that man does of his own free will turn to God, cannot have been taught of God, for that is one of the first principles taught us when God begins with us, that we have neither will nor power, but that He gives both; that He is "Alpha and Omega" in the salvation of men.[8]

The Calvinist Flaw

The Calvinist is right in attesting that salvation is God's business, from beginning to end. Let's give the Calvinist some credit for understanding sovereignty. Like Martin Luther and the early reformers, the Calvinist recognizes that human willpower has nothing to do with salvation in the least. If self-effort is involved, it is not grace. That's Gospel truth.

But hold the phone ... before we all join a Southern Baptist church and hand trophies to the Calvinists, let's follow their

---

[8] Charles Spurgeon, "Free Will a Slave." (1855 Sermon)

THE ELECTION OF JESUS CHRIST

claims a bit deeper. There is also a fatal flaw in the Calvinist camp. If God is completely sovereign in the salvation business – then how does the Calvinist explain the fact that some people are clearly *not* Christians? Faith is a gift from God. Okay. So why doesn't everyone have it? If man can take no credit for his faith – should man likewise be blamed for not having any faith at all?

If God is sovereign over all matters … who is to blame for those who don't have faith?

Over the centuries, reformed theologians pushed John Calvin's beliefs into areas he never fully embraced himself. They edged into what is commonly called "hyper-Calvinism" or "federal Calvinism" – from which emerged the despicable doctrine of *double-predestination* (also called "limited atonement"). For God to be sovereign, they say, He must sovereignly choose those who will be saved … and consequently, he also *chooses those who will be damned.*

The hyper-Calvinist therefore could not admit that Jesus died for everybody … instead, He just died for the "elect." The atoning work of Christ was "limited" for the saints only, and doesn't really apply to the damned. Their idea of double-predestination is this: Since God is fully in charge of a Christian's salvation (even choosing to save them before they were born), He must likewise be in charge of an unbeliever's damnation (also damning them before they were born). They rightly believe that God is in control, not man. They rightly believe that willpower does not save you – God does. But the logical conclusion that followed is that God must also "choose" some people *not* to be recipients of salvation. His sovereignty must mean that God *chooses* to hate some people and to send them to Hell – absolutely apart from their own human say in the matter. Forget blaming Adam or the devil … for the hyper-Calvinist, it is God Himself who is mankind's worst enemy – sending untold billions of people to roast forever in Hell!

THE ELECTION OF JESUS CHRIST

Wait ... did you just say God *chooses to hate* some people? Not all Calvinists would say it that way. But a hyper-Calvinist who is honest about his theology will. Puritan revivalist Jonathan Edwards in the most famous sermon ever preached on American soil, *Sinners in the Hands of an Angry God*, puts it this way, "The God that holds you over the pit of Hell, much as one holds a spider, or some loathsome insect over the fire, abhors you, and is dreadfully provoked: His wrath towards you burns like fire; He looks upon you as worthy of nothing else, but to be cast into the fire; He is of purer eyes than to bear to have you in His sight; you are ten thousand times more abominable in His eyes, than the most hateful venomous serpent is in ours."

Does that sound like the heart of Jesus? Intentionally choosing to send some people to Hell before the foundation of the world? God is not the enemy of the damned; He's the Savior of the damned. The last time I checked the scriptures, I read that "God so *loved* the world that He gave His only begotten Son ..." (John 3:16).

Humanistic Focus

And so the theological battle continues ... The fatal flaw of the Arminian is that he relies on human willpower to save himself from Hell (and often *maintain* that salvation on his own). The Arminian god at least gives a fair shot to everyone, but ultimately he is impotent. The Arminian god is not sovereign – he stops at the threshold of man's willpower. He knocks at the door, but it is up to *you* to open up for salvation. The fatal flaw of the hyper-Calvinist on the other hand (who is right on many other points) is that he blames God for intentionally choosing billions of people for Hell.

In the one camp, salvation is up to *you*. In the other camp, salvation is a gift of God ... yet he maniacally withholds it from most people! You have a choice between either an impotent sissy god or an utterly demonic one.

The Arminian has an in-turned, navel-gazing approach to

THE ELECTION OF JESUS CHRIST

salvation – constantly striving to make sure he's in the club. But don't think the Calvinist is immune to navel-gazing. He's always looking over his shoulder to make sure he's done enough good works to "verify" he has been limitedly atoned for – that he is indeed a persevering saint who really received irresistible grace.

If you're not confused by now, you should be. Both Arminianism and hyper-Calvinism are humanistic theologies – based more on logic than centered on the person of Christ. The Arminian relies on his "self-choice" or "*human* decision." The hyper-Calvinist thinks God is randomly picking certain individual *humans* to save or burn at the dawn of creation: "This human is going to Heaven. That human is going to Hell!" And by statistical historical odds, most of mankind was chosen for Hell! For the Calvinist, nobody deserved salvation anyway, so God is just showing off His mercy by saving a few lucky souls ... in fact He *shows off* by tormenting the rest of them forever.

Christ the Elect
The idea that God specifically chooses certain men to be *vessels of destruction* or *vessels of wrath* is a grossly misunderstood reading of Romans chapters nine through eleven. If the Calvinist misconstrues these passages, it must be stated that the Arminian usually ignores them altogether (perhaps for fear the Calvinists are right?). The aim of this book is to take a deep look into these very passages. Does God really choose certain people to hate and destroy?

The hyper-Calvinist idea of double predestination, of God intentionally choosing countless billions to fry in their own fat forever in Hell, is perhaps one of the most despicable theologies ever invented by man. Not only are you working your tail off to make sure your quota of good works proves you to be among the elect – there's a more gaping flaw here. The whole theology makes God worse than the lowest serial killer, rapist or child molester on planet earth. More maniacal and genocidal than Hitler and Vlad the Impaler put together. But the hyper-Calvinist tells you just to live with it! "His ways are higher than

THE ELECTION OF JESUS CHRIST

our ways." ... Really? The Calvinist paints God, not sin, to be the worst enemy of mankind.

But God is not arbitrarily making decisions for or against certain individual *humans*. He did not have a big lotto wheel in the sky deciding which humans would be included. In the beginning, God did not have a random word. No arbitrary word. His word of salvation was not a word of haphazard chance. The word was not "this guy versus that guy."

In the beginning, the Word was "Jesus Christ!"

Jesus Christ is the Word of the Father. Get ready for a mindbender here ...

It is time we put Jesus Christ right back in the center of our understanding of election! It is Christ Himself who was the Decree of the Father at the dawn of creation. He is the Word. He is the Chosen One! He is the Predestined One! He is both the Elector and the Elected. All of our ideas of election must be changed and re-grounded in the Father's election of Jesus Christ. Jesus is God's elected choice *for* humanity. He is both the electing God and the elected man. In reading Ephesians chapter one above, we often forget to notice that our own personal election is always tied first and foremost to God's election of Christ. We are chosen "in Him," predestined "in Him," elect "in Him." For some reason, the *in Him* part is always left off in this theological duel. He does not choose us independently of Christ. No, it is Christ who was chosen, therefore all of humanity was chosen in Him. Just as all died in the first Adam, so all are represented in the Last Adam.

> *For as in Adam all die, so in Christ all will be made alive*
> (1 Cor. 15:22, NIV).

A concept of Christ's vicarious humanity – His representation of the entire human race – is sorely lacking in the Western church. Our Orthodox brothers in the East understand it a bit better. But

THE ELECTION OF JESUS CHRIST

to suggest that all of mankind is somehow mystically included in the humanity of the Chosen One Jesus often opens you to the accusation of Universalism – or that you're suggesting no one goes to Hell, yada yada yada ...

The fact is, most of the church is already to some degree full of Universalists: they believe everyone universally dies in Adam ... they just can't stomach the idea that everyone is likewise universally included in Jesus. In the apostle Paul's latter years, he hammers home this universal scope of the Gospel – that Christianity is not just one flavor in the Baskin Robbins ice cream shop of world religions. Paul understood that there was a very cosmic, catholic (i.e. universal) nature to what Jesus did.

Not only does Paul tell us that Jesus "fills everything in every way" (Eph. 1:23), but that:

> ... by Him all things were created: things in heaven and on earth, visible and invisible, whether thrones or powers or rulers or authorities; all things were created by Him and for Him. He is before all things, and in Him all things hold together (Col. 1:16-17, NIV).

Where are you held together? *In Him!* Where are unbelievers held together? *In Him!* Where is the devil held together? We won't even go there ... but you get the picture. All things are somehow held together *in Christ*. There's nowhere you can run where He doesn't exist. David says "if I make my bed in Hell there you are" (Psalm 139:8). Paul clearly declares to unbelieving pagans on Mars Hill, "'For in Him we live and move and have our being.' As some of your own poets have said, 'We are His offspring'" (Acts 17:28). Even unbelievers are included in Christ in a hidden way – whether or not they know, live it or enjoy the fruit of this marvelous inheritance. Christ was elected not for some, but on behalf of all humanity.

A History of Election
All of scripture is full of election – full of His divine *choosing*. Not

THE ELECTION OF JESUS CHRIST

God's election of Ned Flanders over Homer Simpson. In every Biblical case of God choosing one man over another – it was always a picture, a shadow of God's election of Jesus Christ.

For starters, Adam was the one "elect" man who represented all of humanity ... all men came from him. His sin affected *all*.

There was another choosing as all of humanity was again narrowed down to Noah (the eight in the ark). His chosen seed would represent and repopulate the entire human race. Later, in Abraham, another election was made. And from his loins, yet another election as Isaac was chosen over Ishmael. Next, Jacob's line was chosen over Esau. Don't get mixed up here. Don't think of God *literally* hating Esau and loving Jacob. He hated what Esau represented ... the old man/the sinful self. Scriptures also show God abundantly blessing Esau in another phase of life, as Esau's face was "like seeing the face of God" [Gen. 33:10]. Each of us has played the role of both Jacob and Esau. These men served symbolic roles. They symbolized overarching realities of our old and new nature. Moreover, they point to Christ, who would be the ultimate vessel of honor as well as the vessel of wrath). Even the occasional Old Testament verse indicating that "God hates sinners" must be cast in the light of God's unconditional love of humanity seen in Jesus. God doesn't hate anybody. He hates that old sinful false identity. But the True Self in Christ is your authentic image and identity that even preceded fallen Adam.

The concept of *election* continued as the nation of Israel was God's chosen people. Yet here we have missed the point again. Israel was elected not just for *herself*. Israel was not chosen *apart* from the nations. No, Israel was the chosen on *behalf of all the nations*. "You will be a light to the nations ... " (Gen. 12:1-3). Israel was not for herself alone. She was to point all humanity toward God. We see that Israel – in and of herself (unfortunately like the Church today) displayed no more real integrity or morality than the world around her. Israel obviously failed in her purpose – but God never failed in His!

THE ELECTION OF JESUS CHRIST

The process of election continued. Within Israel's own history, there was a further narrowing down and electing within her ranks through many captivities, exiles, backslidings and wars – the people of God are sifted down to remnant after remnant after remnant throughout the centuries. And all the way through, there were shimmers and glimpses of something God had been scheming all along behind the scenes.

Finally, in the fullness of time, all of this choosing, sifting, electing, narrowing down ... it boiled down to one person. Jesus Christ emerged on the scene. Not just as any man. Jesus Christ arrived as the *One True Israelite*.

Every divine choice of God was ultimately pointing to this ... the one Man Christ. The Representative Man. What T.F. Torrance called *The Vicarious Man*. The Man who would not merely come as the One - but He would also step in as the substitute for the many. The One who represented all Israel and therefore all the nations.

The Light to the Nations
Consider Christ as the true Israelite. Just like Israel, He was sent to Egypt as a child (Matt. 2). Then, like Israel, He was brought back through the waters (Matt. 3). Like Israel, He went into the desert for temptation (Matt. 4). And like Israel, God gave the law through Him (Matt. 5-7). Throughout the Book of Matthew, you see a progressive theme of Jesus portrayed as the one true Israelite – the elect Chosen One. He was God's representative of the entire nation and therefore God's representative choice *for* all of humanity. He was the true Light to the nations. But He was not just any man – He is the God-Man, the incarnation of God Himself – coming to do what mankind could never do. Dying a death you could never die. Again, the vessel of honor Who was also the vessel of dishonor. The One in and through Whom all Israel would be saved.

When we see election through the person of Christ, we see that God is not expecting our willpower to drum up salvation. Jesus

THE ELECTION OF JESUS CHRIST

Christ, the God-Man, became our human response to the Father. It's not about my altar call, but about His own call to the altar. Likewise, when we see election through the person of Christ, we see that in His sovereignty, He is not randomly picking one person over another. His choice is for Christ – therefore His choice is for all of humanity.

> *Consequently, just as one trespass resulted in condemnation for **all people**, so also one righteous act resulted in justification and life for all people. For just as through the disobedience of the one man the many were made sinners, so also through the obedience of the one man the many will be made righteous* (Rom. 5:18-19).

God's choice of election was narrowed down to such a degree that everybody was excluded except for Jesus! "God particularizes salvation, first in Israel and finally in Jesus, precisely in order to universalize it. He cuts out everybody, just so He can eventually draw in all. He excludes, but only to catholicize," writes Robert Capon.[9]

All Have Died
It is one thing to believe Jesus died as a man. There's an untold dimension of *grace when you realize* He came to die as *mankind*. The apostle Paul was literally "standing outside Himself in ecstasy" (2 Cor. 5:13), because he had realized this: "that if one died for all, then all were dead" (v. 15).

> *For since death came through a man, the resurrection of the dead comes also through a man. For* **as in Adam all die, so in Christ all will** *be made alive* (1 Cor. 15:21-22).

Perhaps I'm a broken record – but when the scriptures say *all*, they really do mean *all*. How many died in Adam? *Ummm ... all?* Well we're talking about the exact same *all* here made alive

---

[9] Fr. Robert Capon, Hunting the Divine Fox (Minneapolis, MN: The Seabury Press, 1974), p. 103.

THE ELECTION OF JESUS CHRIST

in Jesus Christ. How quick we are to have faith in the one man Adam to bring death to all ... yet how fearful is the suggestion that the one man Christ could bring life to those same dead men! Again ... some rabid evangelical may call you a *Universalist!*

It is now impossible to see insiders or outsiders. All are included in Christ. In Him even the pagans live and move and have their being ... they are His "offspring." And again, Peter speaking to unbelieving Gentiles said, "You are well aware that it is against our law for a Jew to associate with or visit a Gentile. But God has shown me that I should not call anyone impure or unclean" (Acts 10:28). That's right ... *he said this to unbelievers*. None are to be called impure or unclean. Even unbelievers are included in Christ in some mystical way. Titus 3:2 tells us to "speak evil of no man."

I have a list of scriptures in the next few sections that could cause some folks to get quite angry. Again, the word Pharisee means "separatist," so any notion of God including more people in His plan than we first realized could cause some feathers to get ruffled. I would encourage you to first read through all these verses. Try to keep your anger vented toward the scriptures, and not at me.

The Inclusion of Humanity
For starters, we see that "God was in Christ reconciling the cosmos to Himself" (2 Cor. 5:19). And in Jesus Christ, all things are already forgiven, reconciled and beloved of God:

> *and through Him to reconcile to Himself* **all things**, *whether things on earth or things in Heaven, by making peace through His blood, shed on the cross* (Col. 1:20).

> *to be put into effect when the times reach their fulfillment –*

> *to bring unity to* **all things** *in Heaven and on earth under Christ* (Eph. 1:10).

THE ELECTION OF JESUS CHRIST

Everyone is included in the cleansing work of Christ. We can no longer use a language of exclusion. The outsiders have become insiders. There is no longer "forgiven versus unforgiven." Heaven and Hell are both full of forgiven sinners. I don't even like to say "saved versus unsaved" because that word *saved* means a lot of different things to a lot of different people. About the best we can accurately say is "believer or unbeliever." Do you realize what He's done for you? Do you believe the truth about your inclusion?

> *So insiders and outsiders are both related to God in the same way – through Jesus Christ and His death – and there's no room for hostility. For Christ came to proclaim the unity of all mankind, both to those who were near to God and those who were far away. Through Christ both sides have come into a close relationship with the Father. ... The revealed secret is simply that the outsiders are now insiders sharing in the inheritance, the family, and the promises which come from Christ's message of good news about God* (Eph. 2:16-18; 3:4-6, BCJ).

God has clearly reconciled, redeemed and unified all of humanity in Himself. How does this cause you treat the waiter, the cabbie or the parking attendant? Are they potential Hell fodder, or members of the family who do not yet recognize it?

Christ's work on your behalf is true, whether or not you are aware, whether you feel it or not – even if you don't believe it! Facts are facts, whether they are believed or not. This is objective truth. The believer is a man who, by faith, subjectively recognizes what has happened and therefore enjoys his participation in it. But our acceptance or rejection of Christ's loving sacrifice does not nullify its cosmic scope. Jesus Christ "is the Savior of all people, and especially of those who believe" (1 Tim. 4:10). No matter how much you reject Christ, He never fails to love and include you. You are free to reject Him – but your rejection does not nullify His inclusion of you. You cannot dictate His character that way. You cannot make Him cease

THE ELECTION OF JESUS CHRIST

being Love. At the height of Israel's rejection of their own Messiah, they reached the point of crucifying Him – and yet this was the very act by which He chose to forgive, include and save them all.

A Salvation for All?
The idea of inclusion is scandalous. Hyper-Calvinist Jonathan Edwards demonstrates his schizophrenic theology in this way. On the one hand, he says that God is Love. In fact, he says God is an infinite, inexhaustible resource of pure love. Let's keep it there Jonathan. But no, in his next breath, Edwards literally says that God *hates* sinners with a "hatred apart from love." Really? Hatred apart from love? God does not merely love as an action. If so, then He could possibly hate. No, *God is Love*. All He is capable of is love. Even His wrath is simply a hot extension of His love. It is a big "No!" against sinfulness itself, because of what sinfulness does to destroy and molest His children. Even His wrath is positively *for* you. It's not about His narcissistic anger toward rebels. I don't know anything about "hatred apart from love." The scriptures are clear:

> *For God so loved the world that He gave His one and only Son, that whoever believes in Him shall not perish but have eternal life. For God did not send His Son into the world to condemn the world, but to save the world through Him* (John 3:16-17).

And God specifically loves sinners, as "God demonstrates His own love for us in this: While we were still sinners, Christ died for us" (Rom. 5:8).

Who is this sacrifice for? Jesus Christ is *"the atoning sacrifice ... for the sins of the whole world"* (1 John 2:2). He is the "Lamb of God, who takes away the sin of the world" (John 1:29).

> *For the grace of God has appeared that offers salvation to all people* (Titus 2:11).

THE ELECTION OF JESUS CHRIST

Even in the Old Testament it was foretold:

All the ends of the earth will remember and turn to the Lord, and all the families of the nations will bow down before Him (Psalm 22:27).

Will that literally happen – will *all* turn to the Lord? We will see. We know that God's patience toward sinners is *unlimited* (1 Tim. 1:15-16). And "people are not cast off by the Lord forever" (Lam. 3:31).

In light of what we have seen, consider this verse anew: "Therefore, there is no condemnation for those who are in Christ Jesus … " (Rom. 8:1). Who all is included in that? Well … it's starting to look bigger than we realized.

Often you've heard John 12:32 translated this way, "when I am lifted up from the earth, will draw all *people* to Myself." But in fact, the word "people" is artificially inserted here. Jesus says simply He will draw "all." All of what? In context it says:

"Now is the time for judgment on this world; now the prince of this world will be driven out. And I, when I am lifted up from the earth, will draw all to Myself." He said this to show the kind of death He was going to die (John 12:31-33).

Jesus is saying that in being lifted on the cross (the kind of death He would die), He would drive out the devil (the prince of this world) and draw "all *judgment*" upon Himself … for every last human being on the planet. The *all* is deliciously vague here. All judgment? All people? All the cosmos?

In Luke 23, Jesus said *"Father forgive them. …"* He didn't say, "forgive some of them," or "forgive them if they ask for it" or "take it back if they don't ask for it before they die." From His perspective, everyone is forgiven. That is, of course, if the Father answers Jesus' prayers. Do you think those in Hell are unforgiven? Those in Hell simply refuse to accept their already

THE ELECTION OF JESUS CHRIST

given gift of acceptance.

God's Desire for All

We see in the scripture that the Lord *wants* all men to be saved.

> *The Lord is not slow in keeping His promise, as some understand slowness. Instead He is patient with you, not wanting anyone to perish, but everyone to come to repentance* (2 Pet. 3:9).

> *(God) wants all men to be saved and to come to a knowledge of the truth* (2 Tim. 2:4).

But is He able to do it? We'll see …

> *I know that You can do all things; no purpose of Yours can be thwarted* (Job 42:2).

> *Nothing is too hard for You* (Jer. 32:16).

How big is the family? Did you know that *everyone* is related to Him?

> *Do we not all have one Father? Did not one God create us?* (Mal. 2:10)

> *… I kneel before the Father, from whom every family in Heaven and on earth derives its name* (Eph. 3:14-15).

We know that Philippians 2:10-11 says, "at the name of Jesus every knee will bow, of things in Heaven, and things in earth, and things under the earth. And every tongue will confess that Jesus Christ is Lord, to the glory of God the Father." But Romans 10:13 also says, "Everyone who calls on the name of the Lord will be saved."

But don't put those two verses together!

THE ELECTION OF JESUS CHRIST

Or how about Revelation 5:13 which says, "Then I heard every creature in Heaven and on earth and under the earth and on the sea, and all that is in them, saying: 'To Him who sits on the throne and to the Lamb be praise and honor and glory and power, for ever and ever!'" Here, we see every creature – even those under the earth – worshipping the Lamb. But we are told that those who are in Hell are "forced" into subjugated worship of the Lamb, right? Forget about Matthew 15:8-9, where Jesus says, "These people honor Me with their lips, but their hearts are far from Me. They worship Me in vain. ..." Now we have a forced system of hypocritical worship in Hell?

A Bigger Perspective
Now you could jump to many conclusions after this last section. Let me say this very clearly:

I am not a Universalist. But I do have *hope.*

Let me set your mind at ease by saying I am not clipping out any verses about Hell. But I would ask you (if preserving Hell is your main concern), which of these preceding universal texts do *you* want to clip out of the Bible? Funny how the universal texts always get sidelined in the Western evangelical world, while the Hell passages always get front and center stage.

I am not writing off Hell. I probably believe in Hell more than most people do. But Hell is not God's punishment of sinners. Hell is the condition of unbelief itself ... the very thing He came to save us from. As C.S. Lewis says, "The door of Hell is locked from the inside." You seem to have liberty to stay there as long as you want. But from God's side of the equation, the gates of Heaven are always open day and night (Rev. 21).

To suggest personal decision or faith is unimportant is a misnomer. Of course faith is important! But faith is not the self-willed magical potion that saves you. Faith is simply the recognition that Christ and Christ alone has already died to save you. In fact, the scriptures say it is grace (the free gift), not

THE ELECTION OF JESUS CHRIST

faith, which saves me. Faith is the simple trust and recognition of that salvation. Faith is what causes it to manifest in my life.

For it is by grace you have been saved, through faith – and this not from yourselves, it is the gift of God (Eph. 2:8).

Let's stop looking inwardly, gauging our own faith levels and instead look at Jesus the Author and Perfecter of our faith. "If we are unfaithful, yet He remains faithful" (1 Tim. 2:13). We are not even saved by our own faith, but by His faithfulness. What does this new lens do for us? For starters, we begin to see that God is not "against" any sectors of humanity. He loves all equally and died for all equally.

Not Universalism
As I have stated, as soon as anyone begins to expand on the huge, universal consequences of the atonement ... someone will be quick to label him as a "Universalist." That term means lots of things to lots of people, but Wikipedia is not the best place to learn theology. So I would suggest you do your homework and read your Bible a bit before you start labeling people and throwing big words around! Not every label fits our snap judgment.

For starters, if you boast in a victorious cross, some people think you are throwing away concepts like Hell. "What are you doing with the Hell we know and love?" Other people assume that you are saying "all roads lead to Rome" or that since everybody is "covered" it's not important what you believe, what you do with Jesus or how you live your life. Of course, no one approaches the Father except through Jesus! Also, we must never write off the fact that this Gospel must be *personalized* in the heart of everyone who believes. Faith is vitally important, but we must recognize that faith is a gift, "this is not of your doing" (Eph. 2:8). *The Gospel does not demand faith; the Gospel supplies faith.*

Like the late Fr. Robert Capon, I should more accurately

THE ELECTION OF JESUS CHRIST

describe myself in this way: *I am and I am not a Universalist.* If you're talking about what Christ did to suck up the sin of the entire cosmos in His death on the cross ... then yes. Label me. I am a Universalist. He defeated Hell and the grave once and for all. But if you're talking about writing off the existence of Hell ... then no, I am not a Universalist. As Capon said, "I take with utter seriousness everything that Jesus had to say about Hell, including the eternal torment that such a foolish non-acceptance of His already-given acceptance must entail."[10]

But along with Capon, "I will not – because Jesus did not – locate Hell outside the realm of grace. Grace is forever sovereign, even in Jesus' parables of judgment."

Reason for Hope
I don't know why some men are faithless. Perhaps there is no logical answer for the origin of something as illogical as the evil of unbelief. I do know that in some way, every man is given a measure of faith (Rom. 12:3). I do not know if all men will one day recognize their acceptance by God in this life or the next. But I'm not looking for some future reconciliation to happen. The world has already been reconciled 2,000 years ago at the cross. I'm just hoping they all realize it one day!

Often our questions in this area are simply bad questions. They become problem-oriented and causal-focused. It's better to take a positive approach. Instead of asking why some people don't believe, let's just recognize that Christ has finished the job and know that we have faith to give away! We've been entrusted with a ministry of reconciliation, like Paul, proclaiming that God has reconciled mankind. As they accept the fact, they will experience it. We can leave the rest to God.

Unlike the forever debating Calvinists and Arminians, I am okay to say "I don't know" about some things. I can leave it in the

---

[10] Fr. Robert Capon, *The Romance of the Word: One Man's Love Affair with Theology* (Wm. B. Eerdmans, 1967), 9.

THE ELECTION OF JESUS CHRIST

dialectical tension of mystery. You can make a strong biblical case for "rigid infernalism" (people literally burning forever in literal flames). And you can make a strong scriptural case for the salvation of all men. Christian mysticism can take you where intellectual theology never will. I can live in the tension of not having all the answers – because *the Answer has me*. All I know is that God is *for* all of humanity – so don't paint Him out to be a sadistic torturer of souls. I am not a dogmatic Universalist, because just like the other theological camps, Universalists also rely on logic – drawing hard lines about the future that we cannot accurately predict. I would never make the claim that Hell doesn't exist and write off all those scriptures. But at the same time, I refuse to write off all these clearly universal texts that we've mentioned above. You can make a solid scriptural case for Hell. And you can make a solid scriptural case for Jesus saving the whole universe completely. Instead of writing off one or the other, let's live in the tension of mystery, while maintaining a brilliant hope of a victorious future.

Capon also writes, "The rule in theology is: When you've got two truths which you can't hold in harmony, you don't solve the problem by letting one of them go. You hang on tight and hold them both in paradox. At least that way you don't end up sweeping jewelry under the rug in the name of compulsive neatness."[11]

While I am not a dogmatic Universalist, I will boldly admit that I am a "hopeful." That means I have a strong hope that everyone will eventually give up on their self-imposed Hell (attempting to own something He's defeated). I'm not going to blame God for their Hell. Hell is the self-destructive consequence of not trusting. It's rejecting your already-given gift of acceptance. Either way, the love of God is ultimately inescapable ... you'll either embrace it or you'll hate it. C.S. Lewis says the fire that lights up Heaven and Hell is the same fire – the fire of His love. Let's not swim against its eternal current.

---

[11] Capon, *Hunting the Divine Fox,* p. 95.

THE ELECTION OF JESUS CHRIST

While I have hope, I do not veer into dogmatic assertion. We need the humility of saying "I don't know." The early Church fathers maintained the "possibility" but never the "presumption" of the salvation of all men. After you've died and come back, then you can teach me a thing or two. But until then, all of my Universalist and non-Universalist friends will just have to stay mad at me for remaining a mystical agnostic on this one! In the meantime, I'll keep preaching this glorious Gospel to all who have ears to hear – and those who accuse me of evangelical apathy for this universal hope can attempt to match my record on the mission field.

I would argue that hope is not merely allowed … *it is commanded*. Even God has this hope, wanting none to perish. If you actually *want* people to go to Hell … if you actually want people to fry in their own fat … well, guess where you're probably headed yourself? God has this very same hope for a *catholic* salvation, as He is "not wanting anyone to perish, but everyone to come to repentance" (2 Pet. 3:9). And again, God "wants all men to be saved and to come to a knowledge of the truth" (2 Tim. 2:4).

But we cannot allow our talk of election to devolve into a "Heaven or Hell" issue as theologians have wrongly done in recent centuries.

When it comes to election and Christ's work on behalf of humanity, *Trinitarian theology* is often confused with Universalism by those who are "quick to nullify the Word of God for the sake of tradition" – such as their traditional view of Hell (Matt. 15). To recognize that a loving Father identified Himself with us through the incarnation of His Son – as His eternal crowning goal – is radically inclusive. The fact is that God is not a distant, aloof, solitary monad God in the sky who demands human appeasement. He is a relational love between a Father and a Son in the Spirit. He is other-giving love. And it was always His intention to include the human race into His divine family. In the incarnation, He has forever identified Himself with

THE ELECTION OF JESUS CHRIST

the human race. He has determined not to be God apart from humanity. The Gospel is not that you invited Jesus into your life, but that He has already invited you into His life – to participate forever in the Glory of this Father-Son relationship. And He poured His Spirit out upon all flesh, whether we realize it or not.

SECTION 2. VESSELS OF HONOR AND WRATH
THE LIE OF DOUBLE PREDESTINATION

DOES A SOVEREIGN GOD CHOOSE PEOPLE TO BURN?

For God has bound everyone over to disobedience
so that He may have mercy on them all.
- Romans 11:32

VESSELS OF HONOR AND WRATH

In order to confirm God's choice for humanity in Jesus Christ, we must reconcile this with the one of the main New Testament passages on the topic of election or predestination – Romans 9-11. Remember that this is very simple stuff – it's ultimately about Jesus Christ being the Elect One. The Vicarious Man chosen for all of humanity. But we have to take this slow, because we've been indoctrinated in a Gospel of exclusion our entire lives. In these passages the scriptures talk about God's wrath, His hardening of men's hearts, choosing certain vessels of destruction, etc. We are so quick to jump back into an "insider versus outsider" mentality – a God who sovereignly *chooses* certain men for Hell.

If you are not familiar with Romans 9-11, you may want to read through it before you go further into this chapter. We have included the full text from the NIV at the back of this book (see page 89). When Swiss theologian Karl Barth released his bombshell commentary on the book of Romans in the early 20th century it was a massive break from hundreds of years of thinking that had dominated the Church's understanding of election. Barth is viewed as the most prolific and arguably the most important theologian of the past five centuries. His massive, 13-volume, six-million-word treatise *Church Dogmatics* is a huge, daunting, even *gross* amount of writing. At times you find a single footnote that takes up 20 pages of fine print! *Church Dogmatics* takes up an entire shelf on my bookcase. I don't claim to have spent the two years it would require *just to read it.* Nevertheless, Barth is so full of revelation and insight it would be a huge mistake to overly simplify him and categorically label him as a "Universalist" as a way to avoid digging into his work – as some have mistakenly done. It is Barth's understanding of election that truly sets him apart. In a simple sentence, Barth shows how election is completely summed up in the person of Jesus Christ.

VESSELS OF HONOR AND WRATH

There are a couple of common misunderstandings about Romans 9-11. First, it is not about God *excluding* certain people. These passages are actually about *inclusion!* Secondly, Paul is not dealing with the perceived unfairness of God's wrath toward sinners. He's talking about the unfairness of God's grace toward sinners! The main question is ... *how can grace be fair?* The issue of wrath is just a side note that Paul also clears up.

Paul's Rabbit Trail

Let's put things into context for starters. As Robert Capon points out, these three chapters in Romans are literally a rabbit trail as Paul jumps from "nothing can separate us from the love of God" (Rom. 8:39) up to "all of Israel will be saved" (Rom. 11:26). A rabbit trail you say? Well, of course it's an *inspired* rabbit trail, but a rabbit trail nonetheless. As we know, many of Paul's letters were transcribed as he verbally dictated them. And like any preacher, there are occasions while he's speaking that he rambles off from the main theme ... Case in point being 1 Corinthians 1: "Thank God I didn't baptize any of you guys ... Well, I did baptize Crispus ... Oh, and then there was Gaius ... And, okay I did baptize everybody at Stephanas' house ... Man, I can't really remember if I baptized anybody else? Forget it – the whole point is that I didn't come to baptize but to preach the Gospel!"

Similarly, in Romans 9-11, Paul is building up to the main point that God saved all of Israel in Christ. But Paul doesn't give us a straight shot to his point – he takes a lot of dodgy back alleys to get to this final punch line, "God has handed all men over to disobedience that He may have mercy on all men" (Rom. 11:32). As Capon says:

> On the way to that point, he talks himself into one of the most memorable (and for the unwary interpreter, disastrous) detours in the whole of Scripture. All of the raw materials for double predestination – for God's right to condemn whoever he damn well pleases – come pouring out of him: the pot

VESSELS OF HONOR AND WRATH

that can't speak back to the potter, the potter who is free to make vases or chamber pots, and so on. The dreadful doctrine of divine reprobation, therefore, is based on a misreading – not, admittedly, of Paul's actual words, for he did indeed say all those hard things, but of the force of his words in the context of his whole argument.[12]

Inclusion not Exclusion
It helps to remember that all throughout these passages in Romans 9, Paul is defending grace and the inclusion of the Gentiles. Remember Paul's Jewish mindset. He is often addressing Jewish believers, some of whom get frankly upset at the idea of dirty Gentiles jumping in on their promises. Paul uses their own arguments in these chapters to flip the tables against them. It sounds exclusive on the surface – God choosing Moses over Pharaoh, Isaac over Ishmael, Jacob over Esau. But his Jewish listeners would have *loved this stuff* at the time!

They liked that God chose Moses over Pharaoh (the legal ruler over Egypt) – because Moses was on *their team*. It showed that God didn't need to play by man's rules.

They liked that God chose Jacob over Esau (the rightful firstborn heir) – because Jacob was on *their team*. It showed that God didn't need to play by man's rules.

By man's tradition, Pharaoh should have won the day. But God broke tradition. By man's tradition, Esau should have received the inheritance. But God broke tradition. "Yes, yes! God can break man's rules," the Jewish listeners would have agreed. You may wretch at the idea of God hardening Pharaoh as a pawn and "choosing" Pharaoh against his own will for destruction, but the Jews in Paul's day would have loved this

---

[12] Fr. Robert Capon, *Kingdom, Grace, Judgment: Paradox, Outrage, and Vindication in the Parables of Jesus* (Wm. B. Eerdmans, 1985), p. 365.

VESSELS OF HONOR AND WRATH

idea. *Who cares about Pharaoh, as long as we get the perk package – we're on the receiving end of blessing!*
Paul has his listeners in the palm of his hand. Then, BAM! He flips the tables on them:

"Okay, God can break man's rules and bless whoever He wants? Fine, then. He's giving the dirty Gentiles the same inheritance that you get! He's putting you all on the same level." What Paul is actually saying here is that Pharaoh and Esau get in on the party too! Suddenly the question now becomes, "Is God unjust?"

> *What then shall we say? Is God unjust? Not at all! For He says to Moses, "I will have mercy on whom I have mercy, and I will have compassion on whom I have compassion"* (Rom. 9:14-15).

Those of us raised in the exclusive, separatist mindset of religion tend to read this text opposite of how Paul intended it. We ask, "Is God being unjust by *excluding* Esau?" But Paul is really talking about the unfairness of Esau's *inclusion*. The prodigal son and the elder brother are both received equally. The real question is, "Is God unjust in being good to everybody?" Grace seems immoral ... scandalous!

The religionist doesn't want a God who loves everybody and includes everybody. He likes being an exclusionist. He wants to sit in the VIP lounge by himself.

The Unfairness of Grace

Grace is scandalous because it is undeserved. This question of the flat-out unfairness of grace is the same question Paul has been dealing with his entire ministry in various forms. It was there in the book of Romans since chapter three – the sarcastic argument of Paul's opponents: "If sinners are getting in on this grace free-for-all ... then what are you saying? We should all just sin to our heart's content to the 'glory of God?'" Again, it is brought up at the beginning of Romans 6, "Shall we just keep

VESSELS OF HONOR AND WRATH

sinning then, so that grace abounds?" Paul gives a big emphatic "No! ... You're looking at things backwards!"

In fact, in Romans 9:15 above, people have such a backward perception of God that they immediately try to read between the lines, "God will be angry with whom He will be angry ... He will damn whoever He will damn." But that's not what it says at all. It says He can have *compassion* on whoever He wants – even the undeserving!

867-5309

I could not understand Romans 9 for years. It seemed so harsh to me that God would use even one man – a Judas or a Pharaoh – sovereignly harden his heart then damn him for it forever to accomplish His plans. The Lord progressively gave me revelation on different chapters of Romans in an odd way. Funny as it sounds, like the classic rock song by Tommy Tutone, "867-5309/Jenny" ... I actually understood the chapters of Romans in that exact order: 8, 6, 7, 5, 3 and 9 (I didn't intentionally do exegesis based on '80s pop songs, it just happened that way. So deal with it). Let me explain ...

My appetite was first whetted for the supernatural in Romans 8, as I craved to live as a manifest son of God. I was in a stream of the Church full of guys pushing and striving to kill themselves to climb into the glory of our sonship. But it doesn't work. Next the Lord brought me to Romans 6, where I recommend everyone sit for at least four years. There, I realized I'm already dead. I began soaking continually in the revelation that I have already been crucified with Christ. My sinful nature is already eradicated – there's no struggle to press in for the glory or the supernatural. I'm already perfect from His perspective – believe it or not – and the more I rest and trust in this reality, the more its glory effortlessly manifests. Out of this truth, I wrote my most important book, *Mystical Union*.

By understanding Romans 6, this automatically cleared up Romans 7 – the fighting back of the sinful nature. The fight is over. It's done – dead. I could finally see that Paul was not

VESSELS OF HONOR AND WRATH

wrestling his old nature in the *present tense*. He was merely explaining "as under the law" the impossible struggle for a religionist to be good. Without first reading Romans 6, you can easily isolate the passage of Romans 7 as a present tense reality. But the battle is over. Paul is not a "present tense" Romans 7 man.

What comes next? Chapters 8, 6, 7 ... Now back it up to Romans 5.

Yes, my old nature died with Christ. But this is much bigger than me the believer. Even before he lays into Romans 6, Paul was telling us in chapter five that this death was a reality for *all of mankind*. It is not just me – the individual believer who died with Christ. Jesus didn't just die for the Church – the perfect peaches who would accept Him. He died vicariously as *all mankind*. This scandalous inclusion of all humanity – the heathen, the pagan, the unbeliever – is just as contentious today as it was in Paul's day.

Chapters 8, 6, 7, 5 ... Now back it all the way up to Romans 3 ... It all comes into full perspective. I see that this entire time in the book of Romans from chapter three onward, Paul has been dealing with one huge question ... the *unfairness of grace*.

With this now in full view, I can tackle Romans 9. It is not about some men chosen for Heaven and others chosen for damnation. It is not about Israel versus the Church. It is about the false versus the true identity of all mankind. And it is about the radical inclusion of all men into the gracious plan of God which has been a target of religious criticism from the beginning.

Love of God's People
Let's take Romans 9 right from the top. Paul first notes his sorrow for his fellow unbelieving Israelites, "I have great sorrow and unceasing anguish in my heart" (v. 2). He empathizes with the people of God, just as we can empathize with the religious,

VESSELS OF HONOR AND WRATH

unbelieving church today. Paul was not excluding the Israelites any more than we should exclude ourselves from today's messed up church. As Karl Barth says, lumping Israel and the Church together in this verse, "He does not console himself by supposing the Church to be a human affair of which men can rid themselves."[13] The answer to religion is not to isolate ourselves. We've got to love and deal with religious folks whether we like it or not. This could be the very thing that most cultivates true love in our lives – learning to love those who hate us!

We can empathize with our unbelieving religious brothers, but we should not become so frustrated with anguish that we lose faith. Paul is not depressed. He states in verse six, "It is not as though God's word had failed." For one, he's not surprised at their unbelief. Paul realizes God set the Jews up for failure so that He could redeem them. In the same way, we should not be so frustrated when the Church fails. For all our talk of "advancing the kingdom" or "making revival happen," the Lord allows the church regularly to fall flat on its face. Notice the only time CNN covers the Church is during a sex scandal! We're designed to fail in our religious endeavors. He must allow failure to show our human inadequacy at doing His job. The religion problem keeps us prone to reaccomplish the work He has finished. As Barth says, "The disease from which the church suffers is that God is God."[14]

In verse three, Paul calls these hardened, unbelieving Pharisees his "brothers!" Paul says he was literally willing to be destroyed for their sake. Some translations imply that Paul wished to be "cursed apart from Christ" if it would save his fellow Israelites. Paul obviously knows you cannot trade your salvation for another's. In fact, he just said a few verses earlier in Romans 8

---

[13] Karl Barth, *The Epistle to the Romans*. Translated from the sixth edition by Edwyn Hoskyns (New York: Oxford University Press, 1968), 334.
[14] *Ibid.*, p. 342.

VESSELS OF HONOR AND WRATH

that nothing could separate us from God's love. Additionally, by making this statement Paul is not implying that he loves his countrymen more than he wants to spend eternity with his Savior. This is illogical. The word here *anathema* is key. Anathema can mean "cursed"—but it can also be used in the sense of "devoted to God so as to be destroyed." Paul is expressing a profound love for his countrymen the Israelites, to the degree that he would give his own earthly life to be martyred for them. Consider *Barnes' Notes on the Bible*:

> *The idea, therefore, in these places is simply, "I could be willing to be destroyed, or devoted, to death, for the sake of my countrymen." And the apostle evidently means to say that he would be willing to suffer the bitterest evils, to forego all pleasure, to endure any privation and toil, nay, to offer his life, so that he might be wholly devoted to sufferings, as an offering, if he might be the means of benefiting and saving the nation. ... This does not mean that Paul would be willing to be damned forever. For,*
> *(1) The words do not imply that, and will not bear it.*
> *(2) Such a destruction could in no conceivable way benefit the Jews.*
> *(3) Such a willingness is not and cannot be required. And,*
> *(4) It would be impious and absurd. No man has a right to be willing to be the "eternal enemy" of God; and no man ever yet was, or could be willing to endure everlasting torments. ... It evidently means that he was willing to be devoted by Christ; that is, to be regarded by Him, and appointed by Him, to suffering and death, if by that means he could save his countrymen. It was thus the highest expression of true patriotism and benevolence. It was an example for all Christians and Christian ministers. They should be willing to be devoted to pain, privation, toil, and death, if by that they could save others from ruin.*[15]

---

[15] Albert Barnes, *Barnes' Notes on the New Testament*. "Commentary on Romans 9:3" (Available at www.studylight.org), 1880.

VESSELS OF HONOR AND WRATH

Now if Paul loved the Jews this much, how is it feasibly possible that God would love them any less? And yet the hyper-Calvinist idea of double-predestination states quite frankly that God *hates* these unbelieving, reprobate Jews; in fact, He chose them along with all other unbelievers to go to Hell.

A New Israel

It is not as though God's word had failed. For not all who are descended from Israel are Israel. Nor because they are his descendants are they all Abraham's children. On the contrary, "It is through Isaac that your offspring will be reckoned." In other words, it is not the children by physical descent who are God's children, but it is the children of the promise who are regarded as Abraham's offspring. For this was how the promise was stated: "At the appointed time I will return, and Sarah will have a son" (Rom. 9:6-9).

What's happening here? Paul is stating that there is *another Israel*. There is a spiritual and a natural. The kingdom is not about ethnicity or race. There is a spiritual lineage of those who *believe*. Most Christians understand this concept: that we are true children of Abraham by faith – not by natural Jewish descent.

But here's another spot where religion can send you hurtling toward the wrong interpretation. Paul is not pitting spiritual descent *against* natural descent in such a way that becomes *gnostic* (spiritual things being good and natural things being evil). The two Israels are parallel with the old and new covenants, the old and new creation … The old paved the way for the new. The old was a shadow of the new.

If we are not careful, we can come to some strange conclusions. Natural Jews *versus* Christians. Old Covenant *versus* New Covenant. Your natural life *versus* your spiritual life. None of these are at odds. The former is a shadow of the latter. First the natural, then the spiritual.

VESSELS OF HONOR AND WRATH

What then is really at odds? The *old and new nature*. That which is corrupt versus that which is pure. Creation was corrupted by sin, but it was sin itself — not creation – which must be destroyed. Creation was to be redeemed *from* sinfulness.

Israel was always to be a foreshadow – a picture of the coming new creation. The Promise was not Israel ... Israel was a signpost of the coming Promise. Israel was, in Barth's words, "the womb of the incarnation."

What was brewing in Israel's womb? *Christ, the Chosen One*.

Saved by Election, Not by Works

God was never choosing us based on our ethnicity – and especially not on our good works. Hence, the next verses:

> Not only that, but Rebekah's children were conceived at the same time by our father Isaac. Yet, before the twins were born or had done anything good or bad—in order that God's purpose in election might stand: not by works but by Him who calls—she was told, "The older will serve the younger." Just as it is written: "Jacob I loved, but Esau I hated" (Rom. 9:10-13).

Notice that God's election of Jacob over Esau had nothing whatsoever to do with their performance. Before they were born – before they ever did anything good or bad, God had selected Jacob. The Calvinists are right on this. It is because of God's election – not by works of the law – that we are saved. It is about God's choice alone. But there's a much deeper symbolism here. There is a secret to understanding Jacob and Esau. Something I never saw for years.

Yes, Jacob and Esau were two individual men. But they are something *much more* in this passage. They are *figurative people* – just as Paul used Sarah and Hagar elsewhere as

VESSELS OF HONOR AND WRATH

examples "being taken figuratively: The women represent two covenants" (Gal. 4:24). In the same way, these men are types and shadows of two larger than life realities.

In context of the Gospel, Jacob and Esau depict something bigger. They are not two separate persons – one being the chosen, the other being the damned. Rather, they are two modes of the *same person (your true* nature in Christ or your fallen nature in Adam). Just as they were twins, popping out of the same womb – first the older, then the newer child. They represent two sides of *you!* The old man was destined for destruction on the cross.

Jacob and Esau
Jacob and Esau represent two sides of the same man. The man of faith and the man of unbelief. Even before Jacob realizes his true self in Christ, he looks like Esau. He's dressed in Esau's skin – striving to gain a blessing from his father. His True Self was still hidden under the unbelieving goatskin of Esau - the *fleshly man*.

Forget the idea of human flesh being evil. We're talking about the *fleshly nature* – the old inward propensity toward evil. That's what Esau represented. Whereas Jacob is representative of our new nature – our renewed self in Christ.

Remember the word "flesh" (sarx) is used two different ways. Your human Adamic body is not evil. But the *fleshly nature* – that inward, corrupt propensity toward sinfulness – was the problem. Natural Israel was not evil, but like all of mankind they too needed to be cured of the sinful nature. The Old Covenant was not evil, but its lifeless laws were seized upon by sinfulness and used against us. Your body is not evil, but sin used it as a tool for wickedness. Christ came to liberate us from that nature.

This passage is not about God blessing one individual and damning another. This passage is about our old man versus our new man. Nor is it against Israel – it is against her false identity.

VESSELS OF HONOR AND WRATH

You may say, "Well, that's a stretch! These men are allegories about two different natures?" Of course! Because the *whole premise* of Paul's argument is about true and false Israel. Jacob *is* Israel (remember, he was literally renamed *Israel!*). Israel is both a vessel of mercy and a vessel of wrath in these same passages. Even throughout his individual life, you see Jacob playing a dual role. Jacob is not *simply* the good guy here. Scripture paints Jacob and Esau *both* to be good and bad at times.

> The Sovereign Lord has sworn by Himself – the Lord God Almighty declares: "I abhor the pride of Jacob and detest his fortresses; I will deliver up the city and everything in it" (Amos 6:8).
>
> The mountains melt beneath Him and the valleys split apart, like wax before the fire, like water rushing down a slope. All this is because of Jacob's transgression, because of the sins of the house of Israel (Mic. 4:5).

Here in these verses, Jacob the chosen nation is a *bad boy*. God hates *False Jacob* (his name means *cheat, conniver, swindler*). But whenever there is a name change in scripture, this is significant. It always points to the Gospel transformation. Jacob is renamed *Israel*.

God Does Not Hate Esau

The whole point is that God did not love individual Jacob while hating individual Esau. He loves every individual. But God definitely hates what Esau symbolically represents. God hates *False Esau*. But at the same time, individual Esau also has a *true self* in Christ that bears the very image of God. Remember when Jacob and Esau are reconciled and Jacob says of Esau, "For to see your face is like seeing the face of God, now that you have received me favorably" (Gen. 33:10). When we receive the Lord, the true self emerges.

VESSELS OF HONOR AND WRATH

Was this man Esau, whose lineage God blessed tremendously and whose face was like the very face of God – was he literally hated by God and damned to eternal perdition from before he was even born? No. In a representative capacity, Esau is depicted as an *object of wrath* during his lifetime. But God never hated Esau the man. God doesn't hate anybody. God hates an entity called *Esau* – what Esau represents – *unbelief, the sinful self, the old flesh-driven nature.*

Now does this put some perspective to this entire chapter?

A hyper-Calvinist viewpoint of a sovereign God picking favorites – that we are all just mindless pawns for good or evil – is cruel and whimsical. But it is a different story to see that God didn't literally hate individual Esau from birth – *He hates our old nature*. A nature that is a lie.

Is God Unfair?
Again, we jump straight to the question "is God unfair?" (Rom. 9:14). Was Paul stating this because he really advocated limited atonement? Well if you think God was arbitrarily picking one human over another to go to Hell, then it does seem quite unfair. And Paul's answer seems equally harsh if you're reading it that way. You think he's saying, "God can do whatever He damn well pleases."

On the one hand, Paul is talking about the unfairness of God's mercy. Thus far Paul points out: *It's not about physical descent. It's not about works. It's all about mercy!* And Paul goes into a huge diatribe about the Gentiles getting a gift they weren't even looking for. We're upset because we perceive exclusion here ... but the Jews were upset at the unmerited *inclusion!* Since God can supersede human tradition, human law and human birth order to bless whomever He wants – He's choosing to do so right now by including the Gentiles in salvation. Again, we read, "For He says to Moses, 'I will have mercy on whom I have mercy, and I will have compassion on whom I have compassion'" (v. 15). Don't look at this backwards anymore.

VESSELS OF HONOR AND WRATH

We've used reverse logic to think that He will correspondingly "curse whom He will curse." He's not talking about random selection – the indeterminacy of God's mercy. Rather, this is stating the solid intensity of God's goodness: "I can bless whoever I want! Even the Gentiles!" He is free to pay everybody the same. In fact this verse can be translated as "I am the One who is gracious and merciful!" It's connected to Moses seeing God's glory in Exodus 33:19-20:

> And He said, "I will make all My goodness pass before you and will proclaim before you My name 'The Lord.' And I will be gracious to whom I will be gracious, and will show mercy on whom I will show mercy. But, He said, "you cannot see My face, for man shall not see Me and live."

Even here we see death to self was required. We had to be crucified with Christ to see God's glory. Jacob and Esau represent two sides of the same man: the man of faith and the man of unbelief. One had to be mystically crucified together in the very death of Christ in order for the other to emerge. We are liberated from the old Esau nature to become those people whom Ezekiel prophesied would continually behold Him with unveiled faces (Ezek. 39:29; 2 Cor. 3:18). Not our own "separate death" or "separate cross" – we were baptized into *His death* mystically before we were even born (Rom. 6).

The Hardened Question
This question of fairness has been mounting throughout the book of Romans. Indeed mercy and grace seem unfair. But the question asked by our religious human minds usually comes from the other side of the coin ... What about the *hardened*? The *rejected*? The *not-chosen*? Is it not unfair for a sovereign God to play favorites? What about the *faithless*?

> What if some did not have faith? Will their lack of faith nullify God's faithfulness? Not at all! Let God be true, and every man a liar. As it is written: "So that You may be proved right when You speak and prevail when You judge" (Rom. 3:3-4).

VESSELS OF HONOR AND WRATH

You've got to see that faithlessness has been a problem across the board – for both Jew and Gentile. This question has no bearing on *God's faithfulness*. He is faithful to all. Barth writes:

> *The faithfulness of God may be obscured, but we cannot be rid of it; His gifts may evoke no gratitude, but they will not be withdrawn; His goodness will bring under judgment those who withstand it, but it is His goodness none the less. ... Of what importance is the infidelity of those who have received the grace of God? It preserves and makes known the "presupposition of the whole Christian philosophy" (Calvin). God is true: He is the Answer, the Helper, the Judge, and the Redeemer; not man. ...*[16]

All of Christianity is based on this: That God is right. The fact that we were wrong, unbelieving and sinful only confirms this truth. God is the answer – not our own works! Even our inability to work up faith – our unbelief – has opened us to grace in a backhanded way! It highlighted our need for *God's faithfulness*.

Recognizing that all men were faithless brings either dismay or sheer ecstasy. There is ecstasy in the recognition that all men were sinners because it forces us to lose sight of self and take up the cup of *His salvation*!

> *And I said in mine ecstasy, every man is a liar. What shall I render to the Lord for all the things wherein He has rewarded me? I will take the cup of salvation, and call upon the name of the Lord* (Psalm 116:11-13, LXX).

Our sin (unbelief included) has become an occasion for His grace. What the enemy intended for evil, God used for good.

> *But if our unrighteousness brings out God's righteousness more clearly, what shall we say? That God is unjust in bringing His wrath on us? (I am using a human*

---

[16] Barth, *The Epistle to the Romans*, p. 80.

VESSELS OF HONOR AND WRATH

> *argument). Certainly not! If that were so, how could God judge the world? Someone might argue, "If my falsehood enhances God's truthfulness and so increases His glory, why am I still condemned as a sinner?" Why not say—as some slanderously claim that we say—"Let us do evil that good may result"? Their condemnation is just!* (Rom. 3:5-8).

Human logic says, "Grace is an excuse to sin ... so why not do evil that good may result?" And the human argument also says, "Why therefore should God be judging me if my sin highlights His glory?" The very glory of God is that He is *not* judging you for your unrighteousness! The Judge took your judgment into His own body. "He that judgeth is also He that restoreth all things," says Barth.[17]

> *But now apart from the law the righteousness of God has been made known, to which the Law and the Prophets testify. This righteousness is given through the faithfulness of Jesus Christ to all who believe. There is no difference between Jew and Gentile, for all have sinned and fall short of the glory of God, and all are justified freely by His grace through the redemption that came by Christ Jesus* (Rom. 3:21-24).

Martin Luther says of this verse, "Note that here is the very centre and kernel of the Epistle and of all Scripture." The Gospel does not establish barriers. It breaks them down. It is not about the election of some and the rejection of others. All men were handed over to unbelief ... if He is unfair, then He is unfair to everybody! He has an answer up His sleeve ... but let's not jump ahead of ourselves. Paul gives us a few more theological hurdles before we reach that simple conclusion.

The Potter and the Clay

Let us continue with a stretching passage in Romans 9:

---

[17] *Ibid.*, p. 77.

VESSELS OF HONOR AND WRATH

It does not, therefore, depend on human desire or effort, but on God's mercy. For Scripture says to Pharaoh: "I raised you up for this very purpose, that I might display My power in you and that My name might be proclaimed in all the earth." Therefore God has mercy on whom He wants to have mercy, and He hardens whom He wants to harden. One of you will say to me: "Then why does God still blame us? For who is able to resist His will?" But who are you, a human being, to talk back to God? "Shall what is formed say to the one who formed it, 'Why did you make me like this?'" Does not the potter have the right to make out of the same lump of clay some pottery for special purposes and some for common use? What if God, although choosing to show His wrath and make His power known, bore with great patience the objects of His wrath—prepared for destruction? What if He did this to make the riches of His glory known to the objects of His mercy, whom He prepared in advance for glory — even us, whom He also called, not only from the Jews but also from the Gentiles? As He says in Hosea: "I will call them 'My people' who are not My people; and I will call her 'my loved one' who is not My loved one," and "In the very place where it was said to them, 'You are not My people,' there they will be called 'children of the living God' (Rom. 9:16-26).

Before we jump into the question of Pharaoh's hardening, let us not lose sight of the main point: *It does not, therefore, depend on human desire or effort, but on God's mercy*. The love of God transcends our attempt to earn or even to desire that love.

Let us resist a fear-based interpretation, and rest in His love for a moment. Paul does indeed shift gears a bit now, and he aims this fairness topic a little more toward our misunderstanding of sovereignty. Here we have God hardening Pharaoh. And on the surface, this passage seems a bit dismal. Not the most encouraging analogy: *You're just a lump of clay*. Well, remember that you're the lump of clay that He's married to!

VESSELS OF HONOR AND WRATH

In verse 20, Paul is not saying the pot is "not allowed" to talk back to the Potter. He's saying, "It's not even possible!" Pots don't even have mouths! Who are you to challenge the way God is doing things — as if you've got a better idea? This is a ridiculous impossibility. God is so real and alive that, in comparison, you are like an inanimate object. Yet you are now questioning His goodness? His *goodness* is infinitely higher than yours. Who are we to argue goodness with Mr. Goodness Himself? You are a Mickey Mouse print T-shirt trying to articulate the delight of Disneyworld itself.

This is not a passage stating God is a hard-nosed dictator. He's saying that God is so good you can't even begin to fathom, much less argue that He's unfair. Paul is simply stating that our questioning of God's goodness is juvenile. He is infinitely better than our highest estimation of Him. Whenever you think you're more moral than God, it's time to check the plumbing under your theological sink.

Hardened Only to Include
Allow me to step back and review what we've learned so far.

The question has arisen that *grace is unfair*. This is the Jewish complaint. They liked Jacob being chosen over Esau – but now that Israel is on the short end of the stick (now that she's looking a bit more like Esau and Pharaoh herself), they're starting to ask another question: "How is it fair that a sovereign God should harden anybody indiscriminately?" And that's probably the question that's been bouncing around in your mind as well. So Paul begins to address this issue of God's fairness with three points:

1- *He says that God can do whatever He wants.* Sounds like a fearful truth, and we don't like this answer. But it has to be stated because it's true. God can do whatever He wants.

But if we leave it here (like a hyper-Calvinist), God still seems capricious, maniacal and exclusive. It doesn't answer the

VESSELS OF HONOR AND WRATH

ethical question of God's mercy. How can He select some over others if He is truly loving? So Paul introduces another point:
2 - *He hardens some, in order to bring others in.* Pharaoh was hardened so the Israelites could be liberated from slavery. In the same way, now Israel has been hardened so they would crucify their own Messiah, opening a door of salvation for the Gentiles and any Slick Willie who wants to jump in on the free lunch.

Now this answer is a little more positive. The Gentiles can now come into the Welfare Office for a free check. But it does very little to address our number one concern – isn't God still unfair by intentionally hardening the Jews? Or Pharaoh for that matter? Or Judas? Isn't this still exclusivism?

We're going to have to wait until Romans 11 before the final piece comes together here ... so the suspense is mounting! But I want to take a minute to mention something very simple that, for some reason, is completely overlooked in this passage:

Romans 9-11 has nothing to do with Hell!

Hardening is Temporary

As an evangelical Christian, you have probably just assumed this passage means God hardened Pharaoh and intentionally sent him to the bowels of the underworld with Judas and Nero. Kudos to your human logic. But *Hell* is never once mentioned in this chapter. Pharaoh, Moses, Jacob, Esau, Isaac, Ishmael – all are individual people whose temporal lives served to mirror greater spiritual ramifications for all of us. There is something about a great reconciliation here – where each man plays a different side of the same metaphorical coin. *The old and the new man.* We're looking at a passage where Israel plays the role of both chosen people and the harlot. And ultimately, a bigger picture is forming where Jew and Gentile come forth together as believers to comprise the *one new man*.

VESSELS OF HONOR AND WRATH

"Now, this secret concerns not this or that man, but all men. By it men are not divided, but united. In its presence they all stand on one line - for Jacob is always Esau also, and in the eternal 'Moment' of revelation Esau is also Jacob," writes Barth.[18] The mystery of the Gospel is that vessels of wrath become vessels of honor. Jesus Christ was the vessel of honor that became the vessel of dishonor. Each individual has an Esau who must be rejected by God so that his true Jacob is called forth into inheritance. Jacob is disguised in his brother's goatskin until his true identity is revealed. Every individual (every fallen Adamic man) is an Esau with the seed and image of God – the chosen Jacob – inside of him in a hidden way.

All humanity is united in Christ. Some try to resist it – but your resistance backhandedly proves His love all the more! It further illustrates the depths of depravity He crossed to rescue you. Your sin can't block God's love – it only proves it. This scandalous fact is why Paul is relentlessly accused of preaching "license to sin."

Like Joseph's brothers rejecting him and selling him into slavery, they left-handedly lifted him into prominence as alpha male in Egypt where he would eventually save the entire family ... "What you meant for evil," Joseph said, "God used for good." And later the Jews would crucify the Messiah, unknowingly opening the door of salvation to the world.

The rejected are executing time both their own wicked will and, unbeknownst to them, the gracious will of God simultaneously. You can resist Him all you want, but the only reaction you'll evoke from Him is your inclusion. This is why, when sin abounds, grace abounds all the more.

Karl Barth says there is a "type" of double predestination, but not in the twisted sense we have imagined – both sides are still included "in Him" like it or not. You're either in Him

---

[18] *Ibid.*, p. 347.

VESSELS OF HONOR AND WRATH

experiencing the joys of your resurrection, or you're in Him demanding a reprobation He has already bore on your behalf – fighting against the bottomless pit of love. The fiery pleasure of the love you reject is inescapable and becomes heaping coals on your head.

Regardless, the sovereign inclusion of God's election of us in Jesus invalidates all strife for "entry" into His promises. The Church, not knowing its own identity, is still striving to "become" the Church of Jacob. Wrestling, cheating, attempting to gain its spiritual inheritance through her religious exercises. It goes on in a perpetual fear of Esau – fighting an old nature that doesn't even exist from God's perspective. The Church struggles in a constant fear of rejection and a self-imposed Hell that has been overcome and whose gates cannot contain us. Barth explains:

> For God is the God of Esau, because He is the God of Jacob. He is the creator of tribulation, because He is a bringer of help. He rejects in order that He may elect. We must not avoid the crisis or vacate the two-sided pillar of cloud of its scandal.[19]

God's patient bearing with the vessels of wrath "to an expected end" cannot be seen as contradictory to His predestined favor toward them. God is not double-minded toward men, nor does He have two separate purposes. It's the same purpose. His "No" corroborates His "Yes."

He deals a devastating blow to man's willing and running, no matter how carnal or religious. But hidden in this "no" – in this operation of wrath – God is actually being gracious toward man. God has been saying "no" to Israel throughout her entire rebellious/religious history. But hidden all along in the law and in Israel's failure was God's eternal "yes" in Jesus Christ.

---

[19] *Ibid.*, p. 350.

VESSELS OF HONOR AND WRATH

Just as glimmers of Christ were seen hidden throughout Israel's history – the Rock in the wilderness, the Manna from Heaven – He will not stay hidden forever. God will not leave Him in the grave, but raise Him from the dead. There is a final *revealing*.

If all these scriptures seem abrasive, it is probably because you've been reading them through a lens of self-condemnation. Barth quotes Friedrich Steinhofer in saying, "The more a man finds these texts to be harsh, the more is he wedded to his own righteousness. Inasmuch, however, as he is able to live quietly with them, his heart rests altogether in grace."[20] When you trust God, worry doesn't twist your interpretation. Fear of being "non-elect" is an indication you are already depending on your own self-righteousness to enter the club.

Vessels of wrath are all fit for a temporal destruction. Pharaoh faces a temporal destruction. It says nothing of his eternal destiny. These are not necessarily individuals bound for Hell. Romans 11:25 says the hardening of Israel is "in part." God never destines any man for Hell. And what man has not been like Pharaoh?

All we see from this side of eternity are the temporal dealings of God with man in this life. Men who played shitty roles in God's unfolding drama of human history. Who are we to judge even the final fate of Pharaohs, Hitlers and unchurched aborigines of this world, not knowing their reaction when they one day come face to face with their Maker? Even those horrendously depraved souls from Noah's day have a hope on the other side of the divide. The flood was not the final word for them. Christ is the final Word. Peter tells us that Christ preached to the dead in prison who were "judged according to the flesh that they might live according to God in the Spirit" (1 Peter 4:6). Although it may be evangelical suicide to say this, we know nothing of whether a man may accept the Lord's grace after he dies. The

---

[20] *Ibid.*

VESSELS OF HONOR AND WRATH

hardening of the vessels of wrath here is only "in part." Barth writes:

> *The man that is hardened is the visible man, who ... neither knows or practices repentance. But who among us either knows or practices repentance? This is our hardening. The man to whom God shows mercy is the invisible man, the man who is miraculously united with God, the newborn man whose repentance is God's work.*[21]

The Rejected and Elected are One Man

The contrast between these two vessels is dissolved in God. Barth continues, "If the church desires to be altogether Moses – and what church ... does not so desire? Then it must recognize and ponder the fact that it is Pharaoh, the church of Esau." To recognize our sainthood, we must admit we were also depraved sinners. This is accepting His gift of transformation.

This is a scandal. What happens to the backbone of Israel if the uncircumcision – both Jacob and Esau – can be elect? And what happens to the Church and its mission if God chose to undertake and do Himself the very work entrusted to it?

Take a moment now on your own to read through Romans 10. I won't spend much time with it, because you likely won't have as much difficulty here as in the previous chapter.

In Paul's line of thought it becomes clear that salvation has been offered to all men by no work, no effort of their own. This is foundational Gospel 101. Paul says the Israelites – like the Church today – are zealous for the things of God but their zeal lacked knowledge (Rom. 10:2). What knowledge? The awareness that Christ fully accomplished the job in setting men right with God. *Christ is the culmination of the law so that there may be righteousness for everyone who believes* (Rom. 10:4). There is no differentiation anymore. Salvation is for all who trust

---

[21] *Ibid.*, p. 353.

VESSELS OF HONOR AND WRATH

in faith. But remember, faith doesn't *make* the message of inclusion happen. Faith is simply agreeing that you are included already! Faith doesn't make you elect. It realizes your election.

And by Romans 11:1, Paul clearly states that "hardened" Israel has not been excluded from salvation: *"I ask then, did God reject His people? By no means!"* Paul is clearly talking about natural Israel here (he goes on describing his natural lineage from the Tribe of Benjamin, etc.). This is quite amazing! We know God does not reject "spiritual Israel" (Rom. 9:6). He doesn't reject believers/the Church. But Paul is saying that God has not rejected those who are clearly *unbelievers* – the murderous Pharisees – which flies in the face of everything evangelical religion has taught us.

So too, at the present time there is a remnant chosen by grace. And if by grace, then it cannot be based on works; if it were, grace would no longer be grace (Rom. 11:5-6).

The Remnant

This is not the first time Paul brings up the term "remnant" in these chapters. With *remnants* in scripture we've often thought of a select few who were able to pull their act together and not get destroyed by God. The frozen chosen that God set aside *apart* from the nations. As we noted earlier, Israel was not chosen *apart* from the nations. She was chosen *for* the nations – to be a light to the nations (Gen. 12). Throughout scripture, the idea of the remnant was always a pledge from God that He has not rejected the whole. The few who vicariously represented the many. The 7,000 that never bowed the knee to Baal (1 Kings 19:18). The ten righteous men bargained by Abraham that would preserve the city of Sodom (Gen. 18:32). There weren't even ten, and it was destroyed anyway. But despite this temporal destruction, He says in Ezekiel 16:53, "I will restore the fortunes of Sodom!"

Christ the Vicarious Man was the ultimate Remnant. God's pledge on behalf of humanity. Paul continues in Romans 11:16,

VESSELS OF HONOR AND WRATH

"If the part of the dough offered as first fruits is holy, then the whole batch is holy; if the root is holy, so are the branches." In the old covenant, the first handful of dough was offered to God, which consecrated the entire batch. The *one* makes the *all* holy. A remnant is not the little bit that's kept untainted from the world. It's the little bit that infects the whole world with holiness. True holiness is much more contagious than sin.

> *What then? What the people of Israel sought so earnestly they did not obtain. The elect among them did, but the others were hardened, as it is written: "God gave them a spirit of stupor, eyes that could not see and ears that could not hear, to this very day"* (Rom. 11:7-8).

Israel, in seeking justification by law, did not find it. Some (like the disciples) did through faith. But the others were intentionally hardened and "… their rejection brought reconciliation to the world" (Rom. 11:15). Again, God allowed them to be hardened by a "spirit of stupor" – blind enough to reject and crucify their own Messiah – and the door was opened for all humanity to be saved.

It's Not Your Fault

Paul does not want the Gentiles becoming conceited over this. We can't take any credit for believing:

> *If some of the branches have been broken off, and you, though a wild olive shoot, have been grafted in among the others and now share in the nourishing sap from the olive root, do not consider yourself to be superior to those other branches. If you do, consider this: You do not support the root, but the root supports you. You will say then, "Branches were broken off so that I could be grafted in." Granted. But they were broken off because of unbelief, and you stand by faith. Do not be arrogant, but tremble. For if God did not spare the natural branches, He will not spare you either* (Rom. 11:17-21).

VESSELS OF HONOR AND WRATH

Some of those Jewish branches were "broken off" and the wild olive branches – the Gentiles – were grafted in. But God was not playing favorites in this. It is unbelief – not God's ultimate desire – that precludes the Jews from the promise. He says in verse 23, *"and if they do not persist in unbelief, they will be grafted in, for God is able to graft them in again."*

"Cutting off" language sounds harsh. But it is because of God's goodness that He does not allow us to thrive in our religious self-efforts. He allows us to dry up when we fail to recognize that *He alone* is the source of our sap and sustenance! Some would say we are "grafted into Israel," but Israel is not the root. God is the root that supports the whole. The point is not to be arrogant, thinking we have done anything to earn this but to "be on guard, tremble" ... guard yourself against any self-righteous notions! "Well at least I understand grace!" *No, it's even by grace that you understand grace!*

The cutting off of branches is for their own ultimate good. The hardening is for their own ultimate good. The blinding is for their good! In saying, "He will not spare you," Paul is not saying you will "lose your salvation." You did nothing to gain your salvation and you can do nothing to lose it. But even religionist Christians can become so hardened with unbelief as to "forget" their salvation and no longer taste or experience it.

> *Again I ask: Did they* ("non-elect" hardened Jews) *stumble so as to fall beyond recovery? Not at all! Rather, because of their transgression, salvation has come to the Gentiles to make Israel envious. But if their transgression means riches for the world, and their loss means riches for the Gentiles, how much greater riches will their full inclusion bring!*
> (Rom. 11:11-12)

Paul holds out the very real hope for these unbelieving natural-born Jews that their acceptance of this Gospel will bring resurrection life! Suddenly in a sharp U-turn, Romans 11 starts to become one of Paul's most *universal* texts in all of his

VESSELS OF HONOR AND WRATH

writings. The "non-elect" who have been hardened still have hope!

All of Israel will be Saved

We see in Romans 11 that God's judgment of sin, His severity toward the disobedient and His willingness to blind the eyes and harden the hearts of the reprobate, are signs of a greater fundamental quality: *His loving mercy*.

For if their rejection brought reconciliation to the world, what will their acceptance be but life from the dead? (Rom. 11:15)

Natural Israel's hardening opened the door for the Gentiles. But is that the only final destiny for natural Israel? Or for any of the *non-elect*? There seems to be some mystical hope of resurrection for all. Finally, Paul sums up his entire three-chapter discourse in this scandalous refrain:

*I do not want you to be ignorant of this mystery, brothers and sisters, so that you may not be conceited: Israel has experienced a hardening in part until the full number of the Gentiles has come in, and in this way **all Israel will be saved**. As it is written: "The deliverer will come from Zion; He will turn godlessness away from Jacob. And this is My covenant with them when I take away their sins." As far as the Gospel is concerned, they are enemies for your sake; but **as far as election is concerned, they are loved** on account of the patriarchs, **for God's gifts and His call are irrevocable**. Just as you who were at one time disobedient to God have now received mercy as a result of their disobedience, so **they too have now become disobedient in order that they too may now receive mercy** as a result of God's mercy to you. **For God has bound everyone over to disobedience so that He may have mercy on them all** (Rom. 11:25-32).*

VESSELS OF HONOR AND WRATH

This verse sums up the entire New Testament, "For God has imprisoned *all* in disobedience so that He may be merciful to *all*."

Mercy for All
God is pure mercy. When we recognize and live by faith as the new man (the true self), we experience His mercy as kindness. When we live under the delusion of the sinful nature (in disobedience), we experience this very mercy as severity and wrath. The ones God blinds, hardens or cuts off the vine for a season are the very ones He is merciful toward. His former action toward them (severity) is only understood by looking at His latter action (mercy). His No always points to His Yes. The latter action is the goal of the former. He hands all over to disobedience for the grand triumphal goal of having mercy on every last single one of them.

Real simple. Same gift for everybody.

It's only confusing because at the beginning of Romans 9, Paul is speaking from the perspective of an exclusive Jewish mindset – he uses arguments that appear to endorse the old "chosen few" idea. An ultimate master of wordplay. But he only does this in order to flip that argument on its head. He layers the inclusion of all humanity in the work of Christ. Follow through to the end of Romans 11 and you no longer see God's mercy being withheld either from the vessels of honor or the vessels of wrath.

Now back to our old question of Pharaoh's hardening. Legally God hardened Pharaoh because He can – He's God. But that's not enough for the ethical question of His goodness. He hardened Pharaoh in order to have mercy on the Israelites. That's better, but it's still exclusive – poor Pharaoh becomes a helpless pawn in this whole game!

When God hardened Pharaoh, it showed him the destructive nature of his own sin. It amplified his reprobation to show him

VESSELS OF HONOR AND WRATH

the direst consequences of his corruption. The scriptures say in Exodus 7:5 that God was striking Egypt in order to *reveal Himself to them*. Paul puts the Egyptians and Israelites on the same plane, and God's actions toward them are no different. At the end of the day, there were no favorites. God allowed all the race of Adam to be imprisoned to disobedience, *so that mercy may be shown to them all*.

Who are the vessels of wrath? In Romans 9:22, Paul says the Israelites. *God's chosen people are also the vessels of wrath*! The chosen Jerusalem is mystically called Sodom in Revelation! There is a clear connection here if you have eyes to see it – that the vessels of wrath and the vessels of mercy are the same individuals. He also says, "as regards to election they are beloved" (Rom. 11:28) and that "they have now become disobedient in order that they too might receive mercy" (Rom. 11:31). In Ephesians 2:3 Paul says all Christians were at one time "children of wrath." Paul, once known as Saul (meaning *sheol*, "the grave"), was himself a vessel of wrath.

Since the Pharisees did not recognize their origins in Jesus, He calls them children of the devil. But the devil didn't authentically spawn or create anyone. They originated in God, but were living according to a foreign father. Jesus *came to His own* and they didn't receive or grasp Him.

By shutting sinners up to face the consequences of their own disobedience, God reveals the self-defeating nature of evil and destroys the illusion that makes wickedness possible in the first place. This does not mean God is rewarding unrepentant sinners. It is about transforming and bringing those sinners to faith, where they realize their co-crucifixion and the destruction of their old nature in the cross of Christ.

The Mystery of Inclusion

The entire aim of God's wrath is to show the futility of sin, and to point us to grace.

VESSELS OF HONOR AND WRATH

I do not want you to be ignorant of this mystery, brothers and sisters, so that you may not be conceited: Israel has experienced a hardening in part until the full number of the Gentiles has come in (Rom. 11:25).

I believe one of the reasons these passages have eluded and angered us so much is because of the logic and dogmatism that have been forced upon them. People have blamed God's sovereignty for the injustice in this world, rather than looking to His sovereignty for grand redemptive purposes.

This hardening is "in part." If it is in part, then it cannot necessary be eternal.

"This whole situation constitutes a mystery from which there is no escape. It is of paramount importance that we should not be 'ignorant of this mystery' for it is the God-given riddle, in which we verily encounter God," adds Barth.[22] The whole goal of this hardening (blinding, rejecting) is to cause you to reject your religion. Blinding is the curse of the Pharisee that, like Saul struck on the road to Damascus, he might eventually see.
All Pharisees *choose God*. But there is no eternal security in the passing vapor of human choice or willpower. Luther said, "Men snap at repentance, as a dog snaps at a fly, but it escapes them." Man's effort to ascend to God is the very thing that must be destroyed. Religion is ultimate self-trust and idolatry. In election, we are in no way talking about a man who "chooses" God. As Barth says:

> *This hardening is no more than a temporal condition of mankind. ... The exhaustion of human possibility clearly pre-supposes the possibility of God. The death of the old man pre-supposes the birth of the new. The catastrophe of the Church pre-supposes the breaking forth of redemption. ...*

---

[22] *Ibid.*, p. 413.

VESSELS OF HONOR AND WRATH

The man who selects God must make way for the man who is selected by God.[23]

This is really the only *double predestination* – your human-effort Esau must give way to your already-chosen Jacob identity. It is not to him that wills or runs, but God who shows mercy. Salvation is His business. All we can do is trust that He finished the job.

In Christ, rejection has been swallowed up in election. Christ Himself is the fullness of the Gentiles. He shall turn ungodliness away from Jacob. That is, He peels back the veil of Esau. The death of Jesus unites the elected and the rejected.

---

[23] *Ibid.*, pp. 414-415.

Epilogue

God's predestined intention for you was to lavish upon you the eternal wealth of His goodness. You were created as an object of love. Jesus was not twisting His Father's arm to love you on the cross, acting as a sort of divine lightning rod to absorb the wrath of a schizophrenic deity. That vengeful, legalistic view of the atonement is a modern invention, and not the message of the early Church fathers. The Father was not venting His wrath on Jesus. The Father was venting His love through Jesus. The Trinity was manifesting Its eternal heart of love for you - making clear that the choice of God is positively *for* you – even when you were estranged from Him. Jesus was never the whipping boy of a legalistic Father who demanded the scales of some obscure cosmic justice be paid ... with a resounding "Too bad!" for those who don't catch the message this side of their deathbed. No, God is pure mercy. True justice was His demand that you be restored to your rightful place as an heir of your Father's kingdom. Rather than absorbing the brutality of a capricious deity, Jesus was absorbing the sinfulness of mankind and all its inherent ramifications – destroying our disease in His own broken servant body on the cross. This He did on behalf of humanity.

> *He who descended is the very One who ascended higher than all the heavens, in order to fill the whole universe*
> (Eph. 4:10).

In the incarnation, God bound the created order to Himself. We are all enveloped in Him, as is all of creation – whether we realize it by faith or not. The scripture hints at the possibility that all might come to know Christ, but the mystery remains open ended. Leave room for mystery. We are saved through trusting Jesus, not by figuring Him out.

God cut all but Jesus out of the salvation business. He excluded everybody so He could include everybody. Salvation

EPILOGUE

was never conditioned by our performance – including the "drumming up" of faith. Humanity cannot create or manufacture union with God. We can only discover it. One thing for certain is that we are no longer outsiders. Jesus Christ went to the altar and accepted you into His life. Kudos to our Arminian brothers for at least recognizing a beautiful gift of participation in this divine dance with the Trinity. But this salvation was decided for us long before we ever responded to it. Election is God's solid choice for mankind in Jesus.

To truncate this Message of election to a tract on Heaven and Hell is to sell the Gospel far short of its inherent worth. Our Orthodox brothers in the East are perhaps right in the suggestion that Heaven and Hell are merely our human language to describe what it's like to be in the presence of God ... we all go to the same place, but to some His fire of love is manifest as torment because some demand to reject the inescapable love of God. We are not created to swim upstream of this infinite torrent of love and fight against it. But rather to receive it and give it freely. To be carried along by the unforced rhythms of grace.

In any discussion on election, let us be slow to draw presumptions on the eternal fate of those, whose temporal lives seemed so full of bitterness, hatred and rebellion. Their hardening was to an expected end, that He might show mercy. The cardinal rule in modern American evangelicalism is one must say the sinner's prayer before he dies. But this fundamental truth seems to be curiously missing from the Bible. There is room for hope for all men when they meet their Maker. Perhaps we've underestimated Jesus in this whole equation. As Martin Luther wrote in a letter to Hans von Rechenberg, "God forbid that I should limit the time of acquiring faith to the present life. In the depth of the Divine mercy there may be opportunity to win it in the future." Time will be the tell. Let us not be dogmatic where the scriptures offer a double-sided coin of mystery.

EPILOGUE

In the beginning, God created Adam and put him in a garden called Eden. Eden means "pleasure" or *voluptuous living.* You were created for a life of divine pleasure. Chosen for paradise – to drink from that River of Pleasure that flows at His right hand. This always was and always will be His intent for you. And that Paradise is found only in the revelation of His Son, the unity of God and Man, Who is Eden incarnate.

It was always the eternal plan of God to unite Himself to humanity. To experience the bliss of other-giving love. Therefore, God permanently identified Himself with the human race in the incarnation. "His purpose was to make all history work out towards one culminating moment, when He could bring every movement in the whole universe, spiritual as well as material, to a head in Christ" (Eph. 1:10, WAND). God could not stomach being alone. Because He is Love, He could not fathom an existence apart from you. In the incarnation, He fully embraced the human condition. God and man both find their ultimate fulfillment in the Gospel.

You are more than a created object. You are His very divine, immortal offspring. Otherwise God would be an idolater to love you so. The scriptures tell us that God literally threw Adam into an ecstasy (*tardemah*), and out of his side came forth a bride. In the same way, you were chosen and brought forth from His broken side, the Last Adam, in the ecstasy of His Passion. Brought forth from His very life-giving breath, you bear His very image, worth and affection. Christ is not unequally yoked to His Bride. You are no vessel of dishonor – no chamber pot, no wretched spider or worm. You are flesh of His flesh, bone of His bone. This is the True Self.

The new creation in Christ is not an alternative plan devised by the Godhead after the first Adam failed. God was not wringing His hands, going back to the drawing board after Adam botched life in the Garden and ate the forbidden fruit. The life, death and resurrection of Jesus was not a hurried tourniquet applied to stem the Adamic bleed. Adam's fall never caught the

EPILOGUE

Lord by surprise, and His incarnation was not a Hail Mary pass – no last ditch effort to rescue as many as possible from the unforeseen devastation of the fall.

Hidden even within the collapse of mankind's utter failure was a latent plan to redeem us from that very fall, revealed at the appointed time in the person of Jesus. It was always His intent that out of the old, the new would spring forth. That the seed must die in order to bear fruit. Although evil was allowed to run its course and mar creation, His ultimate predestined purpose was to restore that very creation to something far better than Eden. To return us to the very image of our Creator. Long before Adam ever fell, Christ was the Lamb who was slain from the very foundation of the world. Christ was always the original purpose of the Father. Incarnation was not a patch over fix. It was always the intention of the Godhead from eternity past to step into our humanity. Don't be duped into fearing the G.O.D. preached under so many steeples who amounts to nothing more than a twisted human aberration cast upon the scriptures.

Our Father of infinite freedom allowed His creation to explore to the hilt the delusional idea that there is any existence whatsoever apart from Mr. Existence Himself. He allowed us to run into the bushes in a delusional attempt to escape His presence – to pretend there was a place He didn't exist. But separation never existed from His perspective – in our blindness, the illusion of separation only existed from our end. How much more can we now relish the work of Christ – the Chosen One elected to wake us up from that Adamic fallacy Who became the sacrificial ram in those bushes to cleanse us of a guilty conscience? Forever we shall cherish the reality that He alone is the Way, the Truth and the Life.

All of creation resounds with this glorious good news, that we have been included in the life of God.

The end of the story culminates with a backdrop not unlike the beginning. Again we see a Garden and a River and the Tree of

EPILOGUE

Life. Behold the predestined plan of God: Deity united with humanity. The intent and purpose and scope of the Gospel. God and man forever meshed in unending unity.

He is the Delight of paradise. And to Him, we are the delight of paradise. Unlike the solitary monad god of religion, who doesn't mind being alone – who was alone for all eternity – the Father of Jesus is a God of pure, unadulterated other-giving love. God in relation. In the circle of the Trinity, there is no performance orientation. Jesus is not working off a checklist making sure he has obtained the Father's approval. There is no pretense, no insecurity in this relationship between Father, Son and Spirit. You've been swept into this circle of unconditional love from time immemorial, predestined in Him – existing in His heart and imagination from before time began.

You will never run fast enough, jump high enough or bow low enough to please the solitary sky god who doesn't care whether he is alone or not. But the Abba of Jesus is a far cry from that mythical divine solo being of our fearful fallen imagination. He thrives on the face-to-face interaction of spending Himself on the object of His love.

Our questions have been all wrong ... Never was there an issue of "Am I chosen?" As if God's choice for us was ever in question. The answer to that question is not found in the depth of our conversion experience, the sincerity of our own personal repentance, or the tears and travailing we have spent trying to mend our own sinfulness. Not in some questionable list of good deeds we've accumulated to prove our acceptance in that circle. Nor was it ever a question of a whimsical arbitrary lotto wheel in the sky, "Whom shall He choose?"

The answer is seen most clearly in the heart of the Father, demonstrated in the sacrificial love the Son on our behalf. And the Spirit is awakening us to this love every day. As T.F. Torrance succinctly wrote, "Unconditional grace is too costly, for it calls in question all that we are and do, so that even in our

EPILOGUE

repenting and believing we cannot rely upon our own response but only upon the response Christ has offered to the Father in our place and on our behalf."

God has never veered from His original intent for humanity. The ancients longed to look into our day, to marvel at the ever-increasing glory of our sonship. The Last Adam has restored all things. We are merely rediscovering what always was. And at the final resurrection, we shall fully see that which was accomplished from the womb of the dawn. Our adoption existed in Christ long before we stumbled into the darkness of the first Adam.

It seems to me no wonder that most theology is *apophatic* (telling us what God is "not like"). So much processing takes place regarding sin, the law and our own fallen, subconscious, twisted projections – because we've cast a god in the shadow of our own false personalities. When all we have known is darkness, it seems difficult to comprehend the light breaking through our dimly opening eyes. We have barely understood our separation from that darkness. If we haven't known what we're *separated from*, how on earth will we know what we are *separated to?*

But there is an inherent *knowing* deep within mankind – no matter how suppressed or ignored it may be. A distant remembrance ... an echo of the light of Paradise from which we came. Perhaps in the coming days, that light will be less and less explored through the medium of book and sermon and human instruction, as invaluable as these resources are to us along the way. It will be embraced in the raw, naked ground of contemplative experience with the living Jesus. Perhaps in the full brightness of this Day, we'll see that the shimmer of light that's been glancing through the shadows all along was none other than *Christ in you, the hope of glory*.

You've been elected for the unfathomable destiny of enjoying Him forever.

THE TEXT
ROMANS 9-11 FROM THE NIV

ROMANS 9

Paul's Anguish Over Israel
¹ I speak the truth in Christ — I am not lying, my conscience confirms it through the Holy Spirit — ² I have great sorrow and unceasing anguish in my heart. ³ For I could wish that I myself were cursed and cut off from Christ for the sake of my people, those of my own race, ⁴ the people of Israel. Theirs is the adoption to sonship; theirs the divine glory, the covenants, the receiving of the law, the temple worship and the promises. ⁵ Theirs are the patriarchs, and from them is traced the human ancestry of the Messiah, who is God over all, forever praised! Amen.

God's Sovereign Choice
⁶ It is not as though God's word had failed. For not all who are descended from Israel are Israel. ⁷ Nor because they are His descendants are they all Abraham's children. On the contrary, "It is through Isaac that your offspring will be reckoned." ⁸ In other words, it is not the children by physical descent who are God's children, but it is the children of the promise who are regarded as Abraham's offspring. ⁹ For this was how the promise was stated: "At the appointed time I will return, and Sarah will have a son."

¹⁰ Not only that, but Rebekah's children were conceived at the same time by our father Isaac. ¹¹ Yet, before the twins were born or had done anything good or bad — in order that God's purpose in election might stand: ¹² not by works but by Him who calls — she was told, "The older will serve the younger." ¹³ Just as it is written: "Jacob I loved, but Esau I hated."

THE TEXT

¹⁴ What then shall we say? Is God unjust? Not at all! ¹⁵ For He says to Moses, "I will have mercy on whom I have mercy, and I will have compassion on whom I have compassion."

¹⁶ It does not, therefore, depend on human desire or effort, but on God's mercy. ¹⁷ For Scripture says to Pharaoh: "I raised you up for this very purpose, that I might display my power in you and that my name might be proclaimed in all the earth." ¹⁸ Therefore God has mercy on whom He wants to have mercy, and He hardens whom He wants to harden.

¹⁹ One of you will say to me: "Then why does God still blame us? For who is able to resist His will?" ²⁰ But who are you, a human being, to talk back to God? "Shall what is formed say to the one who formed it, 'Why did you make me like this?'" ²¹ Does not the potter have the right to make out of the same lump of clay some pottery for special purposes and some for common use?

²² What if God, although choosing to show His wrath and make His power known, bore with great patience the objects of His wrath — prepared for destruction? ²³ What if He did this to make the riches of His glory known to the objects of His mercy, whom He prepared in advance for glory — ²⁴ even us, whom He also called, not only from the Jews but also from the Gentiles? ²⁵ As He says in Hosea:

"I will call them 'my people' who are not my people; and I will call her 'my loved one' who is not my loved one," ²⁶ and, "In the very place where it was said to them,'You are not my people,' there they will be called 'children of the living God.'" ²⁷ Isaiah cries out concerning Israel:

"Though the number of the Israelites be like the sand by the sea, only the remnant will be saved. ²⁸ For the Lord will carry out His sentence on earth with speed and finality." ²⁹ It is just as Isaiah

THE TEXT

said previously: "Unless the Lord Almighty had left us descendants, we would have become like Sodom, we would have been like Gomorrah."

Israel's Unbelief
³⁰ What then shall we say? That the Gentiles, who did not pursue righteousness, have obtained it, a righteousness that is by faith; ³¹ but the people of Israel, who pursued the law as the way of righteousness, have not attained their goal. ³² Why not? Because they pursued it not by faith but as if it were by works. They stumbled over the stumbling stone. ³³ As it is written:

"See, I lay in Zion a stone that causes people to stumble and a rock that makes them fall, and the one who believes in Him will never be put to shame."

ROMANS 10

¹ Brothers and sisters, my heart's desire and prayer to God for the Israelites is that they may be saved. ² For I can testify about them that they are zealous for God, but their zeal is not based on knowledge. ³ Since they did not know the righteousness of God and sought to establish their own, they did not submit to God's righteousness. ⁴ Christ is the culmination of the law so that there may be righteousness for everyone who believes.

⁵ Moses writes this about the righteousness that is by the law: "The person who does these things will live by them." ⁶ But the righteousness that is by faith says: "Do not say in your heart, 'Who will ascend into heaven?'" (that is, to bring Christ down) ⁷ "or 'Who will descend into the deep?'" (that is, to bring Christ up from the dead). ⁸ But what does it say? "The word is near you; it is in your mouth and in your heart," that is, the message concerning faith that we proclaim: ⁹ If you declare with your mouth, "Jesus is Lord," and believe in your heart that God raised Him from the dead, you will be saved. ¹⁰ For it is with your heart

THE TEXT

that you believe and are justified, and it is with your mouth that you profess your faith and are saved. [11] As Scripture says, "Anyone who believes in Him will never be put to shame." [12] For there is no difference between Jew and Gentile — the same Lord is Lord of all and richly blesses all who call on Him, [13] for, "Everyone who calls on the name of the Lord will be saved."

[14] How, then, can they call on the one they have not believed in? And how can they believe in the one of whom they have not heard? And how can they hear without someone preaching to them? [15] And how can anyone preach unless they are sent? As it is written: "How beautiful are the feet of those who bring good news!"

[16] But not all the Israelites accepted the good news. For Isaiah says, "Lord, who has believed our message?" [17] Consequently, faith comes from hearing the message, and the message is heard through the word about Christ. [18] But I ask: Did they not hear? Of course they did:

"Their voice has gone out into all the earth, their words to the ends of the world." [19] Again I ask: Did Israel not understand? First, Moses says, "I will make you envious by those who are not a nation; I will make you angry by a nation that has no understanding." [20] And Isaiah boldly says, "I was found by those who did not seek Me; I revealed myself to those who did not ask for Me." [21] But concerning Israel he says, "All day long I have held out my hands to a disobedient and obstinate people."

ROMANS 11

The Remnant of Israel
[1] I ask then: Did God reject His people? By no means! I am an Israelite myself, a descendant of Abraham, from the tribe of Benjamin. [2] God did not reject His people, whom He foreknew. Don't you know what Scripture says in the passage about Elijah

THE TEXT

— how he appealed to God against Israel: [3] "Lord, they have killed your prophets and torn down your altars; I am the only one left, and they are trying to kill me"? [4] And what was God's answer to him? "I have reserved for myself seven thousand who have not bowed the knee to Baal." [5] So too, at the present time there is a remnant chosen by grace. [6] And if by grace, then it cannot be based on works; if it were, grace would no longer be grace.

[7] What then? What the people of Israel sought so earnestly they did not obtain. The elect among them did, but the others were hardened, [8] as it is written: "God gave them a spirit of stupor, eyes that could not see and ears that could not hear, to this very day." [9] And David says: "May their table become a snare and a trap, a stumbling block and a retribution for them. [10] May their eyes be darkened so they cannot see, and their backs be bent forever."

Ingrafted Branches
[11] Again I ask: Did they stumble so as to fall beyond recovery? Not at all! Rather, because of their transgression, salvation has come to the Gentiles to make Israel envious. [12] But if their transgression means riches for the world, and their loss means riches for the Gentiles, how much greater riches will their full inclusion bring!

[13] I am talking to you Gentiles. Inasmuch as I am the apostle to the Gentiles, I take pride in my ministry [14] in the hope that I may somehow arouse my own people to envy and save some of them. [15] For if their rejection brought reconciliation to the world, what will their acceptance be but life from the dead? [16] If the part of the dough offered as firstfruits is holy, then the whole batch is holy; if the root is holy, so are the branches.

[17] If some of the branches have been broken off, and you, though a wild olive shoot, have been grafted in among the others and

THE TEXT

now share in the nourishing sap from the olive root, [18] do not consider yourself to be superior to those other branches. If you do, consider this: You do not support the root, but the root supports you. [19] You will say then, "Branches were broken off so that I could be grafted in." [20] Granted. But they were broken off because of unbelief, and you stand by faith. Do not be arrogant, but tremble. [21] For if God did not spare the natural branches, He will not spare you either.

[22] Consider therefore the kindness and sternness of God: sternness to those who fell, but kindness to you, provided that you continue in His kindness. Otherwise, you also will be cut off. [23] And if they do not persist in unbelief, they will be grafted in, for God is able to graft them in again. [24] After all, if you were cut out of an olive tree that is wild by nature, and contrary to nature were grafted into a cultivated olive tree, how much more readily will these, the natural branches, be grafted into their own olive tree!

All Israel Will Be Saved
[25] I do not want you to be ignorant of this mystery, brothers and sisters, so that you may not be conceited: Israel has experienced a hardening in part until the full number of the Gentiles has come in, [26] and in this way all Israel will be saved. As it is written: "The deliverer will come from Zion; He will turn godlessness away from Jacob. [27] And this is my covenant with them when I take away their sins."

[28] As far as the gospel is concerned, they are enemies for your sake; but as far as election is concerned, they are loved on account of the patriarchs, [29] for God's gifts and His call are irrevocable. [30] Just as you who were at one time disobedient to God have now received mercy as a result of their disobedience, [31] so they too have now become disobedient in order that they too may now receive mercy as a result of God's mercy to you. [32] For

THE TEXT

God has bound everyone over to disobedience so that He may have mercy on them all.

Doxology
[33] Oh, the depth of the riches of the wisdom and knowledge of God!
 How unsearchable His judgments,
  and His paths beyond tracing out!
[34] "Who has known the mind of the Lord?
  Or who has been His counselor?"
[35] "Who has ever given to God,
  that God should repay them?"
[36] For from Him and through Him and for Him are all things.
 To Him be the glory forever! Amen.

ABOUT THE AUTHOR

John Crowder loves to push the envelope and provoke God's people to extreme joy. He is a father and is recognized internationally as an author, speaker and advocate of supernatural Christianity. John is on the forefront of a fresh renewal movement marked by the message of grace, ecstatic experience, miracles and a recovery of the foundational preaching of the finished work of the cross. John and his wife Lily have four children based in Portland, Ore. As founders of Sons of Thunder Ministries and Publications, they speak at schools and conference events around the world. SOT hosts mass evangelism events and operate multiple homes for orphan children in developing nations. They have a background in church planting and currently oversee *Cana New Wine Seminary* in Portland. Along with his bi-annual magazine, *The Ecstatic*, John has written thousands of articles during his journalism career. He has authored six books:

Cosmos Reborn
Mystical Union
The Ecstasy of Loving God
Seven Spirits Burning
The New Mystics
Chosen for Paradise

John's weekly video teachings on *The Jesus Trip* have garnered more than a million views. John and Lily have a heart to see the Kingdom of God manifest creatively in every sector of society. Their vision is to equip the Church and reach the world by clearly communicating the finished work of the cross. Creative miracles and unusual signs and wonders mark John's ministry.

COSMOS REBORN

Did you enjoy *Chosen for Paradise*? Dig further into the topics of this book: the role of faith, the new birth, the vicarious humanity of Christ, Heaven and Hell and many more related themes by picking up our companion book *Cosmos Reborn!*

Christ cured the human condition! Cheer up your theology with a big dose of the happy Gospel! Hardback edition.
$19.95 +Shipping only at **www.thenewmystics.com**

THE ELECTION SERIES

Did you enjoy *Chosen for Paradise*? Dig further into the topic of election, the role of faith, the new birth, the vicarious humanity of Christ, Heaven and Hell and more related series by downloading our five-part audio set *The Election Series!*

Visit our online **Digital Download Store** to get this and other audio teachings from John Crowder at: **www.JohnCrowder.Net**

CONNECT WITH US
SONS OF THUNDER

There are many ways to stay connected with us!

Visit us online at:
www.TheNewMystics.Com

Find out about conferences, mission trips, schools, teaching resources, John's itinerary and more.

Email us at:
info@thenewmystics.org

Write us at:
P.O. Box 40
Marylhurst, OR 97036

Call us toll-free:
1-877-343-3245

Find us on Social Networks:
Facebook: www.facebook.com/revjohncrowder
Twitter: www.twitter.com/thenewmystics
YouTube: www.youtube.com/sonsofthunderpub
Linkedin: www.linkedin.com/in/johnwcrowder
Google Plus: www.google.com/+JohnCrowder

MONTHLY WEB CONFERENCE

Discover our live monthly Web seminar: **The Inner Sanctum**

THENEWMYSTICS.TV

The Inner Sanctum continues to be a fun connection point for Gospel drinkers all around the globe who want to stay plugged in with finished-work theology in an atmosphere of joy and impartation. Members now have access to dozens of hours of archived shows, making it the most comprehensive place to view Sons of Thunder teachings. And each month, John Crowder and guests engage one-on-one with viewers for live teaching and Q&A sessions.

Our Inner Sanctum Web broadcast provides a user-friendly format and we continue to add more interactive features. The Inner Sanctum is also a social media platform where members create a personal profile, share pictures and chat with friends 24-hours a day, even when the show is not live.

Find out about membership for yourself, your church or a home group by visiting **www.TheNewMystics.TV**

THE ECSTATIC MAGAZINE

We produce our bi-annual magazine *The Ecstatic* as a way to bring a cohesive voice to the growing interest in authentic, mystical Christianity – a mysticism rooted in the grace message of Christ's cross – not in dead works, asceticism or external disciplines. In a practical sense, *The Ecstatic* serves as an information gateway to the ministry of John & Lily Crowder. But moreover, it is a first fruit in publishing toward bridging several important themes that are converging at the moment: finished work theology, the miraculous, divine satisfaction and daily human existence in the incarnational life. All of these concepts are intrinsically woven together with contributions from modern writers and ancient voices. A new grace-based, Christ-centered mysticism is on the rise. It is bridging many streams. Relevant is its cultural approach. Radical is its Charismatic fervor. Reformative is its theology of grace. These are guiding values of this publication and our own lives. It is a theological journal whose frequency is joy unspeakable.

Subscribe by email to John Crowder's magazine, *The Ecstatic,* to get a free digital delivery: **www.TheNewMystics.com/Ecstatic**

FREE VIDEOS. THE JESUS TRIP

Subscribe to *The Jesus Trip* ... a weekly video teaching from John Crowder. You can join simply by visiting our web site: **www.TheNewMystics.com**. On our homepage, type in your email address and sign up for our weekly newsletter. You'll receive new video links every time they become available.

Or visit: **www.TheNewMystics.com/TheJesusTrip**

Have an iPhone? Get The New Mystics App for videos on the go

DIGITAL DOWNLOAD STORE

Visit our online **Digital Download Store** to get instant audio teachings on many topics from John Crowder at: **www.JohnCrowder.Net**

DIGITAL DOWNLOAD STORE

Visit our online **Digital Download Store** to get instant audio teachings on many topics from John Crowder at: **www.JohnCrowder.Net**

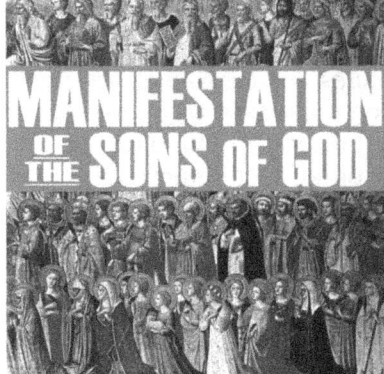

MORE BOOKS BY JOHN CROWDER

Mystical Union
A Scandalous Message!
When you think of the cross, do you think of *fun*? Get ready for the Gospel as you've never heard it. With clear revelatory truths on the New Creation and the scandalous joys of the cross, Mystical Union is one of John's most revolutionary, life-changing works. The happy Gospel of grace is about uninterrupted union with the Divine. This book lays out our most core beliefs. It promises to wreck your theology and cheer you up with undeniable Biblical truths on the free gift of perfection.
$19.95 + Shipping (Hardback)

The Ecstasy of Loving God
Trances, raptures & the supernatural pleasures of Jesus Christ
God has destined you to live in the joyful radiance of Himself, just as Adam was called to live in the realm of Eden. Ecstasy, or "extasis," is the Greek term for trance, and is linked with a pleasurable, God-given state of out-of body experience recorded throughout the sciptures and the Church age. In this book, John takes us on a journey from past to present to introduce us to a lifestyle of a deep practice of God's presence. **$20 + Shipping**

**ORDER AT WWW.THENEWMYSTICS.COM/BOOKS
OR CALL TOLL-FREE 1-877-343-3245**

MORE BOOKS BY JOHN CROWDER

Seven Spirits Burning
The Sevenfold Spirit of God
Seven Spirits Burning, is an extensive, Biblical plunge into the nature and operation of the sevenfold Spirit of God. This book unpackages a deep theological and Christocentric understanding of the seven Spirits. John has taught for years on the topic, and the book stands alone as one of the few detailed compilations of study and experience on this subject. This book could possibly be the *magnum opus* of anything written to date on the Spirit's sevenfold nature. Engage the depths of your union with God.
$19.95 + Shipping (Hardback)

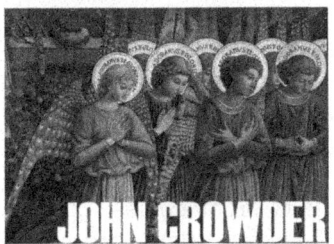

The New Mystics
The supernatural generation
Two thousand years of miracle workers and pioneers crammed into one generation. The fiery bowls of Heaven are being poured out through an extreme body of spiritual forerunners. Are you called to walk among them? *The New Mystics* contains more than 70 photos, illustrations, and biographies of men and women whose lives demonstrated the phenomenal throughout the ages. Let their stories inspire you to join their ranks as part of this supernatural generation.
$15.95 + Shipping

**ORDER AT WWW.THENEWMYSTICS.COM/BOOKS
OR CALL TOLL-FREE 1-877-343-3245**

MORE FROM SONS OF THUNDER

Order More Copies of this Book!

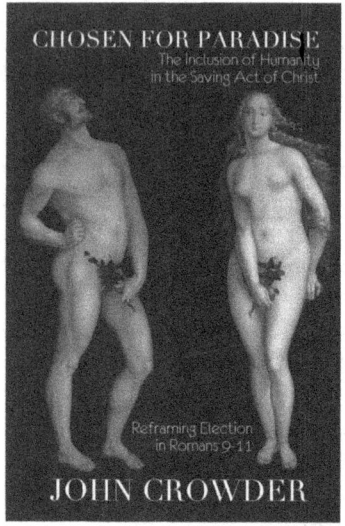

Did you enjoy ...
Chosen for Paradise?
If you were impacted by the revelation in this book, please consider helping us spread the word and share the glorious revelation of the Gospel!

Contact us about bulk order discounts for your friends, church, Bible study groups or even pass it out as a gift to local pastors in your region.

For multiple, bulk order copies, contact us at info@thenewmystics.org. We appreciate your support!

A Brand New Release From Lily Crowder ...

Grace for the Contemplative Parent
Mothers in the Presence of God
Practicing the Presence of God for real-time moms whose lives are full of dirty diapers and soccer practice. This book gives practical, down-to-earth, real-life examples and wisdom from a mother of four. Lily draws readers to the simple awareness of God's presence in the day-to-day role of parenting. Experience fulfillment of a Holy Spirit saturated life in the midst of doing laundry! Realizing the grace of the Gospel and our effortless union with Christ enables mothers to enjoy and rest secure in their spirituality with religion-free parenting.

$14.95 +Shipping only at **www.thenewmystics.com**

CANA SEMINARY

Cana is where the water of the word is transformed into the wine of contemplative experience. Students, pastors and lay leaders who want a grace immersion are invited to participate in this intensive theological training program in a supernatural atmosphere of joy unspeakable.

John Crowder hosts this unique three-month seminary for wild-eyed wonder junkies to be deeply established in the revelation of the Gospel of grace. Cana offers a unique marriage of life-transforming, happy theology woven seamlessly with an intoxicating practice of the presence of God. Where else will you find doctorate level theologians and mystical ecstatics on the same platform? Cana is a drunken seminary. A three-month theological circus of fun geared to saturate students with the Living Word - in the wine of the New Covenant.

More than a ministry school ... Cana is a *Message School*.
www.Cana.Co

QUANTUM CROWDER JOYPOD

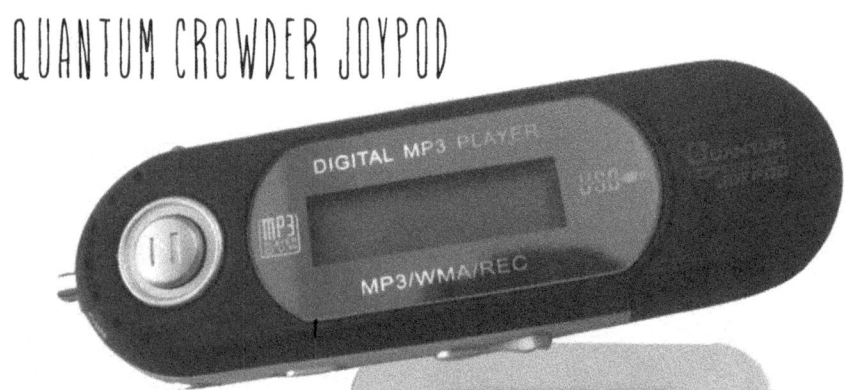

More Than 30 Hours of Crowder in a Can!

The Joypod is a standalone MP3 player that also acts as a flash drive.

Just plug in head phones and listen to 24 full length teachings. Or easily transfer them to your computer or mobile device.

A great gift for Gospel Brain Washing!!

Also includes the full length audio book *Mystical Union* read by John Crowder.

$95 + Shipping
Available at www.TheNewMystics.com
(Contains almost everything from our digital download store … A savings of $40)

PARTNER WITH US

PARTNER
with the Glorious Gospel

When you invest in the poor, the broken and the lost, you are connecting with the tremendous oil of favor, finance and Heavenly provision the gospel has purchased for your own life and ministry. There are abundant awards for those who co-labor together in Kingdom harvest! Reap the nations with us by tangibly partnering with the anointing the Lord has placed on Sons of Thunder. We value your support!

What your support accomplishes:

Housing, Feeding & Schooling Orphan Children
Massive Crusade Evangelism in the Nations
Outreach to the Lepers and Those in Poverty
Equipping the Church with Fresh Revelation
Furthering the Gospel Through Media & Print
Advancing Healing & Miracle Ministry

+ JOIN THE SONS OF THUNDER TEAM!

If you have been blessed by the ministry of John & Lily Crowder and share our same goals and vision, please prayerfully consider becoming a monthly financial contributor. Simply visit us online:

Become a monthly partner at www.TheNewMystics.com/Partners

NOTES